Ragged rhymes and veritable verse

Kevin Vose

A shadow falls on my parchment script,
so I cease my scribbling,
then walk to the ocean to catch a fish,
and scoff it along with garden peas.
Sleepy eyed, I look to the sky for inspiration,
like a sailor expecting a ship.
Come soon please.
Anonymous Celtic poet

Acknowledgements

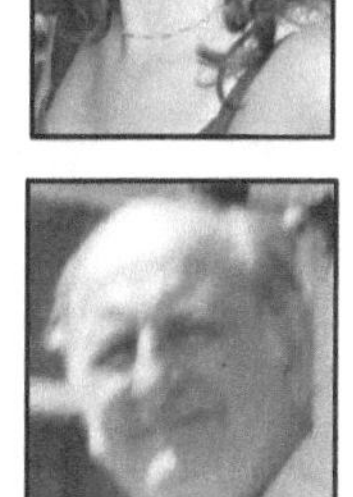

Thanks to Miss Claire Estelle Ashton, *above,* for the illustrations and inspiration, Hove Writers group in the English resort of Brighton, Les Endean, who slightly inspired two poems, *Les – The 'Fool' With The Tool*, and *Les With The Fez*, and fellow old athletes in Blackpool and Liverpool.

Not forgetting my parents, Mary Philomena, *left*, nurse and mother, partner of author and great wit, *right*, John Dennis Vose.

ISBN: 978-81-19654-96-3

First Edition: 2024
Rs. 200/-

Cyberwit.net
HIG 45 Kaushambi Kunj, Kalindipuram
Allahabad - 211011 (U.P.) India
http://www.cyberwit.net
Tel: +(91) 9415091004
E-mail: info@cyberwit.net

Printed at Repro.

CONTENTS

Tree's a crowd

My alter ego and I were wandering through a forest of ancient trees,
tramping through the mulch, making a funny squelching noise,
when he suddenly announced his intention to turn over a new leaf.

Curious, I asked, 'Why a new one?'

For all we could see were old leaves,
which I suggested were due to a raiding party of new-age gardeners
from a commune called Leaf Us Alone.

'Shush,' he cautioned, 'I'm talking to my alter ego,
the pun master Tim Vine.'

He then stroked the ear of a rabbit, commenting,
'We all know that tree's a crowd,' but the poor creature just bared its teeth.

A hare looked amazed that I would allow such a liberty,
for rabbits are gods of the wooded domain,
then loped off into a shadowy enclave, under the branches of a mighty oak.

Under these were a party of ramblers from the
Farlow and District Outdoor Group,
sat on their overcoats made of finest silk.

Milrose Marmite, whom only half the members liked,
had forgotten to put milk in his tea flask, and was milking a cow.
when Mavis Marple, owner of the Delacott Detective Agency,
remarked, 'You're being very bovine.'

'Shush!' said her pal, Beatrice Milady-Mackledow,
and everybody jumped when they heard what they thought
was the voice of BBC radio phone-in presenter Jeremy Vine.

'Beatrice, I'll deal with your text about the right to roam in a minute.

'I'm trying to find a song to accompany it, as I'm a comic, not a disc jockey.

'Before I do that, please tell that chap I want to interview him.
Yes, that fellow standing behind, looking very shy.'

Hearing this, I nudged my alter ego, 'Oh, what it's about, Jeremy?'

But he replied, nonchalantly, 'It's not Jezza speaking, but his comical brother Tim.

'Big bruv's doing a mindfulness session in his potting shed.

'Anyway,' he continued, 'You wrote an article for *Country Walkers' Weekly,* about regenerating soil trod on by ramblers' groups.'

'What?' My alter ego answered, looking at the boot-clad walkers,
'groups like this fine body of outdoor types assembled here whom
I've just spotted dumping banana skins everywhere?'

'Indeed.'

'I think you mean the piece I wrote about the sanctity of forest earth,
entitled *Mulch Ado About Nothing?*'

The radio exploded with, 'I do the jokes!'

My alter ego then laughed uproariously after upstaging that famed punster Tim,
and, turning to walk off, slipped and fell,
which for ever after became a topic to arouse much-needed mirth,
among the Farlow and District Outdoor Group members,
who delighted in seeing my alter ego become the victim of a banana skin.

That was the last I heard of him, although I believe he's now writing scripts
for a remake of a 1970s TV comedy hit called *Monty Python.*

Bus stop love

'I'm indulging in self-pity,' I mused,
reflecting on my latest attempt at seduction,
which hadn't even got past the starting post.

Just like a newly-crowned king on his throne,
I'd had admirers but no partakers in the court of romance.

One particular, dressed so alluring in a nurse's uniform,
used to glance towards me at the bus stop.
However, I was dismayed when I saw her with a
good looking fellow in my favourite pub, The Soho Strumpet.

He spent most of the evening gazing at the television watching cricket,
after she got him up for a bop (and I can swing and step like a good 'un)
and it was obvious that he couldn't even dance.

I'd discovered that many men had cast similar glances at my object of desire,
even a Hong Kong contortionist called the Snap Dragon,
but their affair ended when he called her and said,
'I'm all tied up, I can't make it.'

She told me this story to cheer me as I lay in my hospital bed,
when, after following her along the High Street,
I was knocked down by an ice cream van,
and woke up to see the object of my desire with a thermometer and bedpan.

She asked 'Have you been?'

I answered, bemused, 'Yes, but not a number two.'

'Oh, I'll give you some dates.'

I then asked, 'How's your boyfriend with the muscles?'

She looked surprised, then replied,
'Oh him, he's my personal trainer, but he's as camp as a field of tents.
He's going out with a bodybuilder, and keeps telling me he's in love.'

The next day I saw her at the bus stop and we had lots of the above.

The vanishing island of dreams

She was possessed of a creeping sexuality which slowly
unmasked the innocent – this mysterious woman whom
I met while travelling to Fortopollathrills,
that newly-discovered island with connections to a canary.

The amazing female surprised me by announcing
'They call me Mathematical Millicent.'

But appeared perplexed when I quipped, 'We can count on you!'

I explained the weak joke, and she said,
'Subterranean creatures don't do irony,'
and I wondered what she meant.

As we strolled I gazed at her mouth, smothered in sparkling 'lippy',
and she smiled when I wiped Guinness froth from her lips.

The romantic moment passed when the band came on,
and I tried to impress her by swivelling my hips.

But all she said was, 'I was dancing champion
of the unknown country of Portmacadoo, so I'm not impressed,'
then did another tantalising move,
teasingly asking, 'Why can't you do this?'

I responded with, 'I don't think I'd look good in a dress.'

Then a tall, handsome chap took her onto the dance floor,
and all the men gasped as they caught
glimpses of her well-proportioned calf muscles,
causing a mini-riot, quickly subdued by the bouncer,
a retired former cockney clown known as Cuddly Chuckles.

As we strolled by the shore, Millie stroked a seal,
a cute creature which, in my alcohol-induced imagination,
bore a remarkable resemblance to her.

Alas, as the little mammal disappeared into the depths,
I concluded, we can't always have what we want,
and I was left wondering if Millicent would reappear.

So now, after therapy which has controlled my schizophrenia,
I've left my life as an island-hopping hippy,
and bought a boat with a transparent bottom,
through which I point out the myriad types
of fish in this part of the ocean.

My therapist, whom I'd invited along, declared,
'This reveals wonders nearly as amazing as those geniuses,
James Joyce and Albert Einstein,
whom I firmly believe were on the autistic spectrum.'

Gosh, to think I was paying him for that tripe.

Anyway, the medication he prescribed means I've
forgotten about that woman with the sparkling 'lippy',
who has disappeared into the volcanic earth,
along with that newly-discovered island of Fortopollathrills.

And when I dream of Millie, who vanished in the surf,
I get a dig in the ribs from the missus,
who asks, 'Have you taken your pills?'

A doggy tale

Dog walkers of Brighton look on in awe
when Marianne walks her dogs.

For she is the mistress of the doggie world,
a status that was shattered on the day she met Inspector Cuffem,
the chief cop with a reputation for cracking down on dog owners.

Concern for her charges, Barkalot, Situp and Unbuckle,
caused her to remonstrate, 'Please don't lump me with
all those council-estate doggie foulers.

'My pets are well behaved, they don't bark at postmen and
even stand to attention when the national anthem is played.

'I may be obsessed with all things canine.

'After all, it is my pet subject.

'So, you see I really don't merit a fine.'

At which the policeman gave a stifled chuckle.

'What's more,' she continued, 'I met sergeant Lockemup,
and he said you were always showing
off about your well-bred poodles,
taking them on luxury holidays to Las Vegas.

'You've trained the dogs to operate the slot machines,
after which you make a huge killing by selling your
innocent pets to third-world zoos.'

'So, don't you dare try to prosecute me for not
looking after my dogs' poos'.'

'My dear lady, imposing a monetary punishment was not on my agenda,
just a quiet drink and maybe a waltz.

'I have a private table you know, at a club called The Hacienda.'

'Oh, Mr policeman,' she answered,
'you have caught me at a disadvantage.

'Shall we find a seat and I can eat my lunch?

'Oh, would you like a ham sandwich?'

'Thanks,' he replied with a beaming smile.

'That would be a nice filler before I return to my beat,
the station and its canteen.'

'Oh, do you like the food there?'

'Indeed I do, but...'

'Yes, inspector?'

'They all think I'm a has been.'

She smiled, 'Can you cha cha, you young-looking old man;
I prefer it to a waltz?'

'Indeed I can, in fact I can dance to anything of your choice,
even the cha cha.'

'Great, so I'll see you tomorrow at the aforementioned Hacienda.'

Such is the tale of Marianne, whose partnership
with a canine-coveting cop became the talk of Brighton.

They now live in an isolated cottage underneath Mount Snowdon,
where he acts as consulting detective to the police,

while she runs a rock-climbing course for nimble dogs
who catch the elusive sheep and then covet their fleece.

In time they will enter the Pearly Gates with their
respective pets hard at their heels,
barking and sniffing each other.

For like their owners, they are indeed unlikely soulmates.

The Girl in the Shoe

There is a legend in Cumbria about a girl called Sue,
who had a remarkable impact,
because she took up a strange residence after a giant kicked off a shoe.

The giant's servant, finding his master shoeless,
asked a cobbler to fashion a boot.

When asked how much he wanted for it, the kind fellow,
being from Lancashire, answered, 'Nowt.'

'Just mention me when you dress in your finest suit.'

Years later, a girl christened Susan followed the giant home from a tavern,
and when he fell over drunk, took off one of his boots as he lay spark out.

When a great storm broiled up the Irish Sea with such a force it
even reached the soldiers on the Roman fort at Mediobogdum,
she sailed away inside his left shoe, calling to the servant,
'Go and visit my mum, she quite likes you!'

Sue sailed along but jumped out, disgusted by the pong,
'cos the giant had never washed his feet.

After the sea cleansed the boot she climbed back in,
to be washed up in an Irish cave occupied by the giant Finn McCool,
the one who in a tantrum had picked up rocks and
chucked them into the sea,
thus creating the famous Giant's Causeway off the coast of Antrim.

After she cleaned the place and made him a cup of tea,
Finn unburdened himself.

'I feel self-conscious when I try to chat up girls at the rock pool,
but you've given me confidence with your lovely smile.

'I'll make seaweed porridge, as a thanks for visiting this troubled soul.'

‘Thanks, my mum makes that too,’ she replied,
and invited him to visit her homeland,
recommending a hotel run by MacThistle Musselbank
in the seaside village of Ravenglass.

‘He specialises in catering for big ’uns like you,
with a retractable roof for your bonce.

‘It’s a favourite with soldiers from the Roman fort on
Hardknott Pass, you know,
the one I mentioned in the third stanza,
with the unpronounceable name,
Mediobosgumfus, or summat like that.’

So, with a wave the aforementioned young girl
set off back across the sea.

Nearing home she asked a seagull to fly over and alert her old pal Septimus,
who woke up his boss, the boozy giant, who ran barefoot to the beach.

While gazing to sea he found his left boot thrust into his hand,
courtesy of his servant, who told him,
‘Reach out and scoop her up with your boot.’

‘Thanks,’ Sue squealed, when she landed on the shore.

‘But there was no need to make a fuss.

‘If you don’t mind me saying, I can recommend a herb which destroys foot
odour.

‘Buy it from Proinsias, The Pagan Pongcurer,
if you’re going to pick up damsels with your left boot.’

Then, though the sea was calm, a wave came and swept up the giant’s boot,
depositing it at what is known today as the
aforementioned Giant’s Causeway in Co. Antrim.

Centuries later, tourists explore this legendary place,
imagining themselves back in that distant time when a giant threw
rocks into the sea – and would stop and stare at a large rock shaped like a shoe.

One lady, nicknamed Magical Mildred, who herself was born
in Cumbria and claimed to be able to talk
to wildlife – looked up when an aged seagull screeched,
and amazingly replied in what she claimed was 'gull talk'.

Mildred was so old-fashioned she still insisted
that her children were delivered by a stork.

From that day on the old lady would recount the
tale of the girl from the mountains
who'd sailed to Ireland in a giant's boot, as told to her by a seagull.

'She was a distant cousin, you know,' she told her daughter Constance,
who was full of herself after gaining a first in computer science,
and privately commented that Mildred talked a load of old bull.

But that night there was a terrible storm, threatening to cancel the international
women's rugby game between The Rathdrum Rascals
and The Grasmere Giants.

The next day, the Giants' scrum half, Silky Suzie couldn't find her left boot.

Coincidentally Mildred disappeared, her family discovering her
on the beach next to the rock shaped like a shoe,
holding the player's missing footwear,
gazing forlornly across the Irish Sea,
looking, she claimed, for a girl called Sue.

Constance gave her a right telling off, stomping about,
truly a very annoyed scrum half.

But Mildred reassured her, 'Don't worry,

I’ve banished the spirits over the sea to
my homeland where she has her roots.’

Her daughter groaned, ‘Silky Suzie’s in a bad mood,
as she needs proper, fitting boots.

‘The ref’s threatening to send her off for an early bath,
and the supporters are shouting ‘boo!’

So, Mildred duly returned the stolen item,
and in the second half Silky Suzie scored many tries,
then kicked the winning drop goal with her left foot,
returning a hero to the place that spawned the
legend of the little girl in the shoe.

Old Bore's lament

I'm a talented fellow, full of grandiose claims, my favourite one being
that I've climbed every mountain in England's beautiful Lake District.

So what, I included one which is only a hill, and alright,
I exaggerated when boasting about rescuing that adventurer Ranulph Fiennes.

You know the chap, who walked across Antarctica braving snow and ice?

I didn't rescue him from an avalanche,
or stopped him from plunging over a precipice,
but gave him a lift when I saw him hitching outside Keswick.

This caused an argument at the Hicklegate Hoofers,
led by a guy who insisted on lecturing us at every stop,
so I spoiled his diatribe about lead mines,
subterranean caves and archaeological finds,
by loudly chewing a biscuit.

What a bunch of plonkers!

Though I'm no good on the internet,
I excel at general knowledge – did you
know the Romans brought oats to this country,
thus inventing the healthy dish of porridge?

Or that Hannibal's method of beating off attackers was to
deter his sentries from falling asleep,
by using elephant dung to build fortifications,
causing a terrible pong in the desert heat?

At every opportunity I tell of my achievements – secretary of
Talkative Types Count, a pressure group for those who can't shut up,
and President of North Yorkshire Timekeepers, to name a few.
(If anyone from the latter says I was always late, that's totally untrue).

Everything was going well, until I met that guy, Kevin.

By God! He thinks I'm mentally ill.

Well, he's the one who takes medication for his 'nerves',
depression and obsessive-compulsive disorder.

He even claims I have the latter, what a fool!

This all stemmed from when I wouldn't buy his boots.
Naturally, I'd changed my mind when I discovered he'd worn them,
all he could say was, 'You're beyond the pale!'

Now, the landlord is about to chuck me out,
after I complained, 'That's not real ale!'

What's more, the railway station staff have gone on strike,
saying it's for higher pay, but I've been told they don't
want me spending hours there,
grilling a hapless assistant to get me a cheap train.

That guy I befriended, Kev, whom I used to call a mate,
says he used to be a good long-distance athlete,
but nobody's heard of him, so a woman tells me,
and she's a Hicklegate Park Harrier!

'When I was racing, we ran 70-80 miles a week.
This fun-running lot don't know they're born,'
was his outrageous claim.

Anyway, he's taken to hiding at my approach.
I could see him laughing as the librarian lectured me on being a pain.

Am I the only one who's always asking for wipes to disinfect the keyboard?

Don't go yet, I haven't finished – one more question.
Is there nobody left whom I haven't bored?

Loather the shifty dog

The inspiration for this tale is a little dog called Loather,
owned by a chap called Douglas who,
when I was still employed as a political journalist,
promised he could give me the scoop of my career.

Well, after a few drinks had loosened his tongue,
he surprised me by saying he possessed special powers,
but wouldn't elaborate, hinting at a shady past in Her Majesty's service.

He then shocked me by claiming the canine was also similarly gifted,
even claiming she was a shapeshifter.

When I expressed doubt as to this claim he changed the subject,
talking about his days in North Africa, disguised as a native,
gathering details about enemy infiltrators.

I asked if these were Russians and he laughed,
saying today's villains included a plethora of ruffians,
from New York to Beijing, and that our former allies were often enemies,
disillusioned with hitherto-held values of freedom and
motivated only by the sound of their dirty coins,
sounding – to use a cool term – 'ka ching'.

'Political allegiances,' he claimed, 'just like this magical dog,
can change shape.'

At which I laughed.

He would moan about a former colleague called Maximilian,
who'd retired and was raking it in, while he remained poverty stricken.

Well, it was a sad day when I attended Doug's funeral, but I cheered up after
being told he'd left me his dog.

This coincided with me becoming a comedy writer,
but I was heavily attacked by the right-wing media for
being politically incorrect, with sketches featuring far-right activists
becoming ardent followers of that
example of moralistic cinematic art called Bollywood.

So I took up another pseudonym as Bill Boredgame,
writing in *The Daily Scrivener,*
annoying the 'new literati' – criticising the overuse
of cliches such as 'going forward'.

I was again reviled by a new kid on the block,
Max 'Middleman', a columnist for *The Daily Sketch*,
who hinted that he'd carried out dark deeds in
the service of this disunited kingdom,
which of course he couldn't elaborate on,
as they were covered by the Official Secrets Act.

Then it all went pear shaped, after I claimed in my column,
tongue in cheek, that my dog was a shapeshifter,
I was immediately vilified by rival columnist Maximilian.

The Church of England got on the bandwagon,
with the Bishop of Middleditch slamming me as a believer in paganism.

The opprobrium became too much, with people asking
I and my bemused pet to 'Throw some shapes',
resulting in my resignation from the cushy number on Fleet Street.

Loather then stared at a poster advertising 'Low-fat doggie cakes',
and looked at me (this was after I'd moaned about her getting fat).

I even went to a 'dance your way to fitness' class,
whose promotional material read, 'Get fit and into shape'.

Then one night, as I sat in my garden shed to escape
the baying mob outside my front door – they were a party of Born Again
Christians en route to protest at a controversial London musical in
which God is portrayed as left-wing, and were using me as a protesting-warm-
up – I saw a hairy creature swinging from the apple tree.

'Oh,' I thought, 'that's a first for that bleeding hound, an ape!'
But I cheered up when my pet returned, wagging its tail as if to say sorry for
being naughty.

Then sitting forlorn in the pub I was assured by his
former owner Doug – who'd torn his splendid
waist coat – (he'd insisted on being buried in it)
when climbing the cemetery gates – that I
would get my own back on his old nemesis and now columnist Max,
that retired 'spy, who was also my fiercest critic.

I chuckled when I read what one reporter had written about the furore
surrounding me, 'You couldn't make it up.

'Indeed you could not', I thought the next day
after taking a call from film director Stefan Spellasbog,
asking if I could write a screenplay for his next movie,
Loather The Shape Shifting Dog
(with the promotional material reading
'You won't believe what he'll turn out to be').

Galway Smile

The girl with the Galway smile was giving me grief,
she even thought of being my wife,
but a slim body and a penchant for poetry
couldn't hide her inner cruelty.

She doted on a childhood sweetheart – a financial adviser in the City,
he's known as a character in all the pubs.
But little does she know he's a master thief
who did time in Wormwood Scrubs.

I have trailed her from poetry evenings to meetings
as diverse as Crochet Knitters For Peace,
amateur attempts at the musical *Grease*,
and a Morris dancing convention in Much Salop By The Avon.

While I became a laughing stock at performance poetry evenings,
with my verses about fat women in Blackpool wearing kiss-me-quick hats,
the politically correct audiences who frequent these events,
warmed to her non-rhyming verses to her failed relationships,
while I poured the wine and handed out the biscuits.

But political correction was not on my agenda,
just the girl with the Galway smile who teased
me with her quickstep feet as I fell all over
the dance floor at Walthamstow British Legion,
then sang a song so bitter at Much Hoole Folk Club's
weekly singers come-ye-all evening.

And then as we waited for the bus and
she half-interestedly kissed me for the first time,
I noticed an advert for online dating,
and discovered I could amuse women
with my funny poems.

What's more they rhymed, like the one about a chambermaid easing
an elderly vicar out of her truss.

A year later as I walked down the aisle,
I winked at the girl from Galway who'd suddenly lost her smile.

Walk Under A Cloud

When I was young I breathed the sweet clear air of the Shenandoah River,
then rode through Texas and Montana, in pursuit of a dream as old as time,
of happiness with a loving wife.

But love proved elusive, so I answered the call of
General Custer and his Seventh Cavalry,
and we entered the valley of the Little Big Horn
in the Black Hills of Montana,
where I was lucky to escape with my life.

I woke in a tepee to a see a beautiful Indian girl
whose smile heralded a new dawn.

Walk Under A Cloud was her name,
and she hid me from her tribe, until I,
a shamed deserter, had to escape in disguise,
the only trooper to survive Custer's famous last stand.

Only it was more like a rout, stampeded by
Chief Crazy Horse and his warrior band.

But a decade on I returned to the hills of Montana
and memories of that battle,
back to where memory is so real in a bustling new town,
where lived Walk Under A Cloud,
the beautiful squaw, regarded as a second-class citizen,
but to me she was still the most beautiful Indian girl.

I declared my love with a passion only a
squaw of the Oglala Sioux could equal,
and she returned it, proving she'd forgiven me
for carrying a US Army rifle.

But an ex-cavalry man, Billy Joe McGraw,
took a shine to her as she served chow mein in
Chinese Gordon's Chop Suey House.

McGraw was a boastful fellow who liked to covet Indian women,
and warned me he was a dangerous man to cross.

But Walk Under A Cloud slipped a sleeping herb into his nightly dish,
fearing he would expose me as the coward he'd suspected I was.

But he was so befuddled by the Mickey Finn,
that when he drew his gun I shot him down.
The town proved too hot for us, and we eloped
to the Shenandoah valley.

The girl from the Oglala Sioux found it a strange place.
But in an effort to prove her worth, joined Christians Who Nourish,
a cooking group who conjured up meals for the impoverished of the parish.

The charitable cooks marvelled at her ethnically diverse kitchen,
but when she was out of earshot, gossiped that
it was not 'Christian to marry an Indian'.

But Walk Under A Cloud got her own back,
after she convinced them that drinking the
boiled roots of a cactus was good for digestion,
and would even extend their husbands' manhood.

In fact it did the opposite, leading to deflated egos in the bedroom,
and acute embarrassment when several of the
women emitted excessive flatus.

Many years later I watched as Walk Under A Cloud
was hailed a star of the Wild West's leading circus,
doing somersaults on top of a buffalo.

I, being possessed of a big mouth, became the impresario,
introducing the acts.

These included Sharp Shooter Sam, the expert rifleman,
who could shoot a fly off a prairie dog's tail,
and Bungling Bertram, the hilariously bad magician,
who left the English music hall in disgrace after being
found drunk during the intermission.

But Walk Under A Cloud was the chief attraction,
with a dazzling smile that captivated the young.

They cared not a jot for General Custer, his quest for glory
and the warriors who defeated him in the pretty
valley of the Little Big Horn.

Now we are both old and grey, my betrothed reads
dime novels of when the Indians
chased the buffalo and the Seventh Cavalry
wouldn't leave them alone,
how General Custer did his duty and furthered
the advance of the white man.

But we know the battle at Little Big Horn saw his fall from grace,
and the world looked in awe at the fighting genius,
Oglala Chief Crazy Horse.

His warrior tribe paid the ultimate price for victory,
and I thank God I'd run away,
even though I bore the soldier's stigma of coward.

For I was rescued and loved by an Oglala Sioux,
who became my lovely wife, Walk Under A Cloud.

A game of two halves

Those familiar with Facebook may know the name Fortitude Flickers,
but may not realise that she adopted that moniker after a passionate affair
ended in acrimony.

Under this pseudonym, which gave the normally
shy lady courage she hitherto lacked, Fortitude was invited to
a dinner dance at Old Hovian's Rugby Union Football Club,
where she was introduced to the game of rugby.

Discovering a hidden talent, this plucky lady developed
into a redoubtable fly-half, becoming one of the county's best goal kickers.

Then at a match against the Hastings Harlots, she dazzled a stunned
defence to score under the posts, much to the delight of the county coach,
Horatio Dovecot-Durridge, who had always bemoaned her lack of pace.

However, her online 'friends' still called her a charlatan,
believing she was only sporting behind closed curtains,
but when she scored for England, they were left with egg on their face.

Living in the village of Much-Marching, she became a successful artist,
then delighted her parents by marrying a financial adviser,
one Freddie Flingham, who sold mortgages, ISAs and bonds.

But Fortitude was so bored by him she sought an extra-marital fling,
under her online name of Felicity Frilly Thongs.

You may find her on websites such as Big Smiles And Wide Hips,
Don't Tease Me, Just Please Me, and last but not least, a German one,
Mr Fritz Likes Bulging Lips.

But her bedroom antics grew tiresome, and what's more affected her rugby,
where the splendid kicking which had so marked her game went awry.

One penalty attempt was so bad it hit club president

Brigadier Benson-Bingham (retired) in mid sip of a whisky and soda.

Enter Jarvis O'Dwyer, a tall handsome black African who
had been an upcoming talent at Old Hovians,
until he fell foul of the brigadier after he was heard
condemning Britain for its activities in Africa.

This unpleasantness coincided with the visit of one Jebadiah Johnson,
a professional rugby league talent scout, looking for a player he could recruit.

Told he could be a star and make a fortune, Jarvis was seen with the former,
whose Yorkshire vowels and flat cap drew attention,
and Jarvis was soon told, 'Get rid of that rugby league chap, or you're out!'

Many years later he returned, now a rugby league legend and sex symbol.
Pursued by the media he popped into The Sexy Sculptures Sweet Shop,
where Fortitude was selling her sugary treats.

There he fell for her shy smile and diminutive figure,
declaring himself impressed by her press cuttings and pictures of
try-scoring feats.

However, tongues wagged so much that Fortitude finally told
her husband to stuff his ISAs, bonds and SIPPS,
and went north with Jarvis to his home in Yorkshire,
to join women's rugby league club Keighley Kittyhawks.

At first she struggled to be accepted, but the fans,
led by the chairwoman Mildred Micklewhite, took her to their hearts,
when, encouraged to run with the ball rather than kick it,
she scored amazing tries.

When her fame spread as the girl with the lightning feet who was
spearheading women's sport, she told a renowned sports journalist,
one Sid 'Scribbler' Sullivan, in the saloon bar of the Faltering Fullback,
'There's been times when the decision to kick or run
with the ball became a metaphor for when I could have

fallen down the rapids of life and been dumped on an inhospitable shore..."

Just then Mildred Micklewhite entered the hostelry.
'Oh lass, you'll confuse the poor old chap.
Speak plain, you're in Yorkshire tha' knows, never mind the metaphors."

''Cor,' Fortitude replied, 'I didn't know you knew what a metaphor is for!"

Mildred quickly countered, 'Very funny, that sounds like alliteration.
I learned that at school, where I read about Coleridge, Wordsworth and Byron.

'So stick that up your southern Sussex sophistry.

'That is alliteration, Chairman!|"

'Yes lass, I have hidden depths, even if I am built like a country lavatory."

'Oh, Mildred, I was only kidding.
You were a great player, even if you did, to quote Eddie Waring,
take a lot of early barfs."

Just then Sid coughed and looked at his watch.
'Okay, I'll start again, are you ready, Sid?
To quote some football commentator, it's been a game of two halves..."

At that moment in walked the Keighley Kittyhawks team,
who all chorused, "And the second half's only just beginning!"

Old Farts Harriers

(A harrier is an old-fashioned name for a cross-country runner, and some British athletic clubs still have the title)

I was a Liverpool Harrier, lean and toned to an inch,
then I became a pub drinker and married a woman
who could be described as the original penny pinch.

She loved to entertain with memories of lovers on a far shore,
but when I tried to boast of my athletic exploits,
she pointed to my pot belly,
which had become too big to ignore.

In a vain attempt to boost my manhood I went to a disco,
where I vainly thought my cool haircut would impress the birds.
But my dancing feet did not respond as in days of youth.
Face the facts, I say to myself – you're more at home in the pub,
doing the crossword, now ain't that the truth?

So I went to the line dancing night at the Fiddlers Elbow,
to hear a band called The Chewbaccy Country Cousins
lament – 'Love can prove elusive,
though it's often at your fingertips.

'Cowboys used to buy it for half a dollar, then wake up,
scratch themselves and exclaim, 'I've got nits! Damn that whore!'

So I joined the line dancers, swinging my hips Texan style to an
old thymee beat, reflecting – 'Am I really past my sell-by-date?'

Then I escaped into an imaginary world of The Wild West,
where I, as a smooth-talking gambler
with a wide-awake hat and a gun, shot a crooked sheriff
who tried to throw me out of town.

For I had fallen for his intended – Sally – the owner of the
curiously named Broken Saddle Saloon.
We lived happily ever after in our little home in the west,

where she worshipped my body, and being an artist,
drew shapes on my distinctly un-hairy chest,
murmuring in my ear, 'I love older, down-at-heel men.'

But my dream ended abruptly when I woke up,
after She Who Must Be Obeyed shouted, 'You're talking to yourself again!'

So now, in an effort to gain solace in my dotage,
I joined fellow Old Farts Harriers to reminisce,
taking alcoholic solace at our local, the Duck And Partridge.

We laugh at the overweight chap and his dog doing a park run,
and sneer at so-called celebrities in fancy dress, panting and grimacing,
who say they are running for fun!

For we are the Old Farts Harriers who didn't run for money, but love.
(Granted, we would have cashed in on our talent, such as it was,
but weren't fast enough).

So raise a glass to those old runners who used to
be lean and toned to an inch.

I'll settle back into my dreams of the Old West,
and imagine I'm married to Sally, owner of the Broken Saddle Saloon,
and not her indoors with her tongue that would make a gunfighter flinch.

But like the old cowboys we're too big to sit astride a horse,
and chase the Injuns and outlaws.
Our bellies wobble and we suffer from flatus,
and our personal best times fade into
significance compared to those who weren't similarly blessed.

But we love to indulge ourselves, and recall when we
raced around cross-country courses,
up fells and down dales, for we are the Old Farts Harriers,
so please come and listen to our tall tales.

Flower Power

Flower power erupted in the gardens of Hicklegate,
when an old African lady visited the town's beautiful parks,
and put a magical ingredient on the roots of its budding plants.

She'd obtained it from a mixture of Lesothian beetle droppings,
topping it off with a coating from some Congolese ants.
But former Royal Naval midshipman, Percy Picklethwaite,
smelt a familiar odour, which reminded him of service overseas,
in particular, a war-ravaged, jungly land.

Then, hands a-trembling, he noticed a huge bee,
hovering over a rose, its proboscis ready to spear him.
But the stinger veered off, making a buzzing note he played on his cornet,
for he was a leading member of the town's brass band.

In this capacity he invited an old African lady,
formerly of the British colony of Rhodesia,
whom he'd met that day on a walk in the park,
to accompany the band at their next concert.

For she'd undoubtedly saved him from a deadly sting,
after saying to the hovering buzzer,
'You're only an African killing bee for a fleeting second,
and Percy never hurt the people of Africa.'

'So, please be about your business of pollination,
for the flowers are thirsty for your attention.'

That night she sang a ballad about forgiveness,
then the cornet man remembered how he'd
met this old woman – when as a young man he'd
reached from a lifeboat to save her from the sea.

The band struck up, as its guest singer sang *The Flowers Of The Forest*,
a song Percy had taught her many years before,
as she recovered on the deck of His Majesty's Ship Belfast.

The old sailor burst into tears as the audience cheered,
for a lady who'd put a spell on a Yorkshire park's budding flowers,
and the two old ones rolled back the years.

A mountain spirit speaks out

Rising out of the Ulster coast, I, the mountain God Slieve Donard, greeted you when you returned as a young man, saying,

'Welcome, the faery sentries below warned me of your approach.

As a child, you laughed when told magical creatures
inhabit the mountains of Mourne, my mountain land.

You came once before from that torn city, Belfast,
limping along like a wounded warrior, disillusioned with your prowess,
like the Giant McCool who made a pavement to
nowhere on Antrim's coast.

The guardians of the law chose to inspect you,
suspicious of a stranger at a time of civil unrest,
when you visited the little town of Newcastle nestling below,
with its ice cream parlours and little beach,
just up the road from where 15th-century rebel Phelim O'Neill lies,
contemplating acts of vengeance he committed at nearby Bloody Bridge.

The faery spirits who guard the passes to my kingdom,
as they did when the vengeful Vikings came by flaming boat,
boast that no men with a gun will pass,
whether in masks or the Queen's uniform.

But my faery folk saw a kindred spirit when you climbed up here,
like a messenger from Marathon, so fleet of foot.
I see you've been enjoying the stout, and now more
resemble a country lavatory,
than a chap who ran around the shower to get wet.

So come up through the mist, my spirit will guide you to the top.
Ah, there's a break in the cloud – see out yonder,
where the waves break on that little islet?

That's where I said goodbye to my love, Magwen Bagweal, a Saxon princess.
As I was a true Gael, we were forced by our followers to take sides,
a first example of what historians call a sectarian divide.

As my pal professor 'Fungus' Fergus wrote,
'Hot air is often found around the mouth of a fool,
and we have plenty of them in this divided province.'

Alas, his words didn't go down well among his peers,
and this worthy academic met historian, Leslie Lovelorn,
at a soup kitchen outside Dublin's General Post Office,
its edifice marked by bullets from a great rebellion.

His new friend talked about Ireland's relatively recent clan,
The Midget Murphys.

Originally from the Languedoc region of France,
they encountered the wrath of the bishop,
after nicking wine from his cellar
and selling it to the peasants, thus gaining their allegiance.

His Holiness ordered them thrown off the battlements,
but they bounced off a trampoline,
made from the hides of mountain sheep,
left by devoted followers who rescued their leader,
Fiery Fred Franckenbeans, from the castle's keep.

Fred took his band on a trek across Europe,
where they, among other deeds,
saved a princess from the king of Macedonium,
escaping his wrath by joining a circus,
their acrobatics upstaging the star, Monsieur 'Montrosity',
a fat man whose act involved rolling on the floor to play the euphonium.

Then one night in Vienna they released the animals and took the takings,
sailing down the Danube disguised as a reconstruction of Noah's Ark,
impressing the gullible Venetians.

The Murphs eventually settled in Ireland's county Down,
making a fortune out of the famous shamrock,
which they turned into a saintly source of food,
their exploits giving rise to the expression, still used today, 'Small is good'.

This was just one of many legends told by this odd chap, Lovelorn,
who tearfully described the decline of his professorial career,
which began when he was seen playing in Pontificating Punks,
an alternative Goth band, by the Dean Of Cambridge, The Rev Weepnot-Windblown.

This was bad enough, but when Leslie's wife, 'Flipping' Felicity –
so named due to her habit at Lady Murgatroyd's School For Gentle Girls,
of saying 'flip' instead of the F word, founded lesbian group Fanny's Frolics –
he was out on his ear, the world's most educated bum.

To cheer him up the prof asked, ‘Do you want to meet a mountain God? He resides in that other part of this nation, where the Orange Men march and their leaders proclaim, “Keep out the Pope, or the end will surely be nigh!”’

He answered, ‘If I can get a square meal out of it, I’m game!’

Arriving at a border checkpoint they were escorted to my mountain,
after declaring, ‘We have an appointment with a god over there,
where the magical Mournes meet the heavenly sky.’

Entering my sacred kingdom of Donard with his men,
one corporal McSteake was so infused by the magical air,
that he threw away his rifle to climb my mountain peak.

My faeries were amused by his dialect, Scouse I think they call it.
It was like those sing-song voices spoken in county Cork,
or those residents of the island known as Man,
home to the famous tailless cat.

According to legend, the curious feline hid on a Viking warship,
to escape Polyander Prettypreach, Chief Constable of the animal kingdom,
who had discovered the puss was in love with the rabbit Bunny Boniface,
in contravention of inter-species laws, and condemned her to death.

But she sailed away, hoping to leap onto driftwood
and return to her love nest in the undergrowth.

Seeking a hidey hole in the hold, she disturbed Wolfie Wakeup,
King Shortbeard’s sleepy-eyed Wolf, who grumpily bit her tail.

But the stowaway became one of his majesty’s favourite pets,
after she guided the vessel through fog,
using powers gained from rock pixies,
who’d passed on their echo-sounding powers in
return for keeping the rats down.

Then the pussy spotted a porpoise, Peter Poutalot,
and using sea talk learned from Ollie, the famous juggling seal of Kilkeel,
asked the curious mammal for a lift,
and was deposited on a secluded beach,
with Peter shouting, ‘Sorry I couldn’t get you to Ireland.

‘It’s the Marine Mammals’ AGM tonight, of which I’m chairman.

'Ask for the Isle Of Man's official bard, McGibbins Of The Hill,
whose songs resonate with the hidden aura of his granite abode,
a hollow hacked out of the towering edifice that is Mount Snaefell,
cousin to the supreme mountain god over there in Ireland,
mighty Slieve Donard.'

The former soldier, Corporal McSteake, declared.
'I tell you this tale because it echoes my story.
I discovered the meaning of life can't be found within a uniform.

'For, just like the puss who loved a bunny, I didn't belong anywhere
– a Liverpudlian who hates football, a hippie
who insisted on cutting his hair,
a good-looking fella who rarely got the girl.'

I and this odd chap chatted over several pints of Mournes stout,
myself listing the varieties of turf found on my heathered slopes,
the insects and fauna found within,
such as the fast-spreading Fantailed Fungitude,
kept down by dropping rats droppings from a great height
(my faeries used stilts for this) and the Crawling Cellimus,
a multi-legged Narachnopoid, much sought after by eagles and grouse,
who nest up here to avoid being shot at.

Then the former soldier discoursed about those 18th-century rebels
his Irish granny told him about, who, armed with a pitchfork,
forged their bloody campaigns, while their red-coated enemies
drove a scourge of death from Antrim to Cork.

Then it was time for afternoon tea and a Garibaldi biscuit,
which our guest had nicked from General Bunsonby-Brown's batman,
who at that moment was gazing towards the Mourne mountains,
wondering where that 'bleeding Scouser corporal McSteake had gone'.

Well, dear visitor, I am coming to the conclusion of my tale.
So pleased was I by your appearance I went on a bit,
talking about Vikings, the famous Manx tailless cat and small men called Murphy.

Regrettably, those marvellous beings belong in that nether world,
between the real world and mine.

Alas, when professors Lovelorn and Fergus' claim to have
discovered a mythical god was revealed in *National Geographic Magazine*,
they were devastated by the resulting opprobrium.

So they joined those folkies who meet at Cropredy and Cambridge,
those very 'uncool' festivals, the music there emanating
in the fields and forests of the British Isles,
and not in a house or a garage.

To hear about these and other ancient characters,
my young friend, listen to Lovelorn and Fergus' novelty folk band,
with the former on banjo and himself on fiddle,
cheekily called Much Maligned Madmen,
their lyrics covertly spreading the news
of faeries who inhabit a mountain kingdom in a
green land known to the Gaels as Eireann.

As for the former soldier McSpeake,
he lived in a secret cave in Tollymungin Forest,
and made a fortune busking at the seaside haven of Rockspiddle
(he was too well known in Newcastle),
completing his set with John Denver's hit *Rocky Mountain High*,
enlisting a cat without a tail to go around with the hat,
with the ghosts of those mythical characters, the Midget Murphys,
Wolfie Wakeup and Bonniface The Bunny Rabbit singing the chorus.'

Lament for a fading moon

The British Royal Family have gone, and reality TV has died a death,
my charity-shop clothes are too dusty even for a misanthropic moth,
who flickers as the moon is set to rise,
while that well-travelled Monty Python,
whose surname rhymes with fading,
wonders what will become of Planet Earth.

Meanwhile, two lovers under a fading moon
annoy the romantics by not looking particularly lovestruck,
while cats waking to a rising sun in Spain's twin city of Blackpool,
Benidorm say, in a mournful meow, 'Sod this for a game of soldiers,
I'm off to a hot island with a Canary.

'I'll slip onto a CheapAsChips Flight, that new airline bringing
all these drunks who kept me awake every night.'

Then my Irish mother sets out to haggle at a market stall,
in perfect Spanish, amazing Señor Aficionado with her fluency,
saying, 'Ah, the Irish, they really do love the English.'

These are the memories which in my dotage I strive to recall,
in the midst of yet another cost-of-living storm.

Then my PA looks annoyed, as yet again I kick the waste bin,
full of failed attempts to communicate with a Twittering world.

Dash it, I'll have to pack in this latest attempt at my auto-biography,
Don't Go There!

I only started it on the advice of my publicity agent,
Edward Partyonunaware, whom I've just learned was an
adviser to an ex-British prime minister called Johnson.

I should have known better.
Why, his hobbies include running the Flat Earth Society
and rearing Peckish Polly, a nearly extinct bird.

It's too depressing, so I'll go and look at the moon,
and give the young lovers my blessing.

Dracula is pain in the neck for island's sea mammals

Wandering along the beach I mused to myself,
'What a funny place is this island in The Canaries called Fuerteventura,
with its volcanic rock and crashing surf,
not to mention my eccentric host,
Señorita Marmaduke, who puts garlic outside her door.

'Maybe she thinks we're in that country where a
bloodsucking count preyed on young maidens.'

Of course, I was thinking of Transylvania,
where that dead aristocrat's nocturnal wanderings
nearly sparked a peasants' revolt,
after he couldn't sleep due to woodworm in his coffin.

I soon discovered that King Vladimannanex had acted swiftly
and expelled the count to this remote Spanish possession.

However, word spread of the 'undead' being's imminent arrival,
thanks to author Bram Stoker, who warned the residents to evacuate.

You see, he'd learned of the existence of this fang-laden prowler
from a Transylvanian lady of the night – her cry of,
'I didn't bargain for those size 10 molars, mate!',
alerting the constabulary, and she escaped with her neck intact.

Thus young Bram was inspired to create the legend of Count Dracula.
I laughed after reading about this, before noticing a document
describing a sudden exodus from the island in 1882,
and a geological survey which showed an absence of volcanic activity.

'So,' I mused, 'what prompted their sudden departure?'

Then, arriving in the village of El Cotillo, I asked if there
had been a tradition of undead visitors in the 19th century,
but a bemused mayor denied this.

This was despite graffiti found in a cave on the beach,
saying, 'Dracs woz here.'

'No,' the dignitary said, worried my talk could scare off tourism,
'that's a rumour stemming from a marine biologist,
who was obsessed with Gothic horror films,
especially one featuring Boris Karloff living in a volcano.

'The prof came here on holiday, but left because our
beaches tend to be 'el nudo', and his wife, a lay preacher,
was hit by a bout of prudism.

'He even claimed in our newspaper, *The Canary Islands Clarion*,
that our Monk Seals, a close relative to the Californian short-toothed walrus,
had been found with neck bites.

'He then expounded a theory that they'd been the victim of a vampire,
claiming that a visiting blood-sucking count had,
due to a shortage of humans,
contented himself with what he called 'seal snacks'.

Then on the headland I noticed the skeleton of a whale,
with the inscription,
'It is believed this magnificent creature died from a
wound to the neck – experts are still puzzled
as to the bloodless condition of the corpse.'

That evening I hailed the proprietor, Señorita Marmaduke, who,
her breast adorned with a crucifix,
was cooking a blood-filled stake,
and, with a knowing look, quickly acceded to my
request for a clove of garlic.

Poo! Dung deal for price of a Farthing

Lucinda Make-Piece Farthing lived in India and loved to ride an elephant,
but one day fell off into a pile of dung,
only to be consoled by a little man in a loincloth.

He'd looked at her intensely, then declared,
'I've watched you, and noticed that when our children approach,
you are full of charm, and respectful when we point out,
that sometimes people have to follow their own path.

'For you share our views, Miss Farthing,
and I foretell you'll meet a like-minded soul.

'Now, seeing you discommoded I shall do you a deal.

'Let me spray you with my herbal disinfectant,
made from the root of the Bangalore moth,
and you will appear as a newly-sprung flower that smells so fragrant,
to a man who's waiting for your love.

'But I will do this only on the condition you remember
me as the precursor to a great prophet.'

A brief while later she was hailed by General Montgomery-Hyde.
The distinguished military man recognised her as someone his son,
who was a lieutenant in the Guards,
and at that moment was leading his cavalry troop
in pursuit of a known agitator – had,
before he'd learned of her radical views,
once regarded as a suitable wife.

'Dammit!', he mused, 'she'd even suggested that the natives
were equal in status to us,
and quoted a fellow known as the 'Father of the Mahatma'.

'Why, she'd even laughed at cockney corporal McFloose,
who said, 'Cor blimey, I'd love to make you my struggle and strife.'

After informing the general she was in good health,
he rode some way up the path, glancing behind,

saying, 'Dammit,' he mused, 'she was indeed a good looking woman!'

But Lucinda had hidden behind an ant's nest to extricate
an insect which had invaded her garment,
and on emerging, bumped into a young man.

'How do you do?' Came the charming response,
'I'm Timothy Tickworthy-Hart, but you can call me Tim.'

Lucinda felt there was something not quite right about him,
was it his accent or manner which belied his handsome appearance,
as he backed away from the nest?

He said, 'I say, these creatures are even nastier than my aunts in Blighty.'

'Would you like a cup of tea?' Lucinda asked,
holding out a flask from her well-stocked picnic basket.

'I say Miss, I wasn't really hiding from a tiger,'
Tim admitted later, 'I was having a…

'Oh, I guessed as much,' Lucinda interrupted,
'I was also embarrassed when a beetle crawled up my dress…'

'Do not worry,' cried the young chap, hang on,
I shall take a deep breath before unburdening myself...

'I saw you in the audience when Macaroni's Big Tent
circus visited the village of Much Scratching,
featuring myself, Europe's leading child acrobat.

'You looked dumbfounded at my acrobatic skill,
and the arrow was immediately dispatched from that great being Cupid.'

'Oh, what an interesting story,' replied a stunned Lucinda.

'Do you always talk in para or even full rhyme?'

'Well, I'm influenced by that poet Lord Byron, a known romantic.'

She blushed, 'I am flattered you followed me so far,
and you are indeed quite poetic.

'But I am engaged to Percy Partington-Shand of the Lancashire Fusiliers.
He won a medal in Zululand, gaining the Zulu king's favour
by performing a trick where he ran the gauntlet of an impi's spears,
surviving without a scratch.

'In return he was granted the princess's favour,
a woman he assured me was not at all pretty,
and of course had to consummate the match.

'But it was all part of his duty, and he returned to great acclaim
– while his men were massacred at the battle of Isandwhalna.

'The malicious gossip became too much,
so we sailed to Bombay where he joined the Punjabi Guides,
and he's now far away on a mission to enlist the help of warring tribes.'

At this Timothy sighed and said, almost reluctantly,
'I am afraid I can't compete with such tales of derring do,
I'm only a poor country boy who jumps when people say boo!

'You're talking in rhyme again!'

'Oh sorry, my friend Billy Boyd, whom I met in an Irish bar,
while acrobatting in Stockholm...

'Oh,' Lucy cried, 'a new word, you are clever!'

...'Well, he knows that mind specialist, Sigmund Freud,
who says it's something called obsessive compulsive disorder.

'Anyway, when my father talked of his army days,
it filled him with rare pride, of Salamanca and Balaclava,
but when the recruiting party visited our village, I would run and hide.

'So I became a reporter and met McDougall of *The Times*,
who covered the Zulu War.

'He assured me that your fiancée was indeed a coward.

'Disillusioned, I travelled far and wide,
following the path of Britain's glorious colonial adventure.

'But I became dismayed at its lust for power and obsession with cricket,
and was banned from gentlemen's clubs,
from Bombay to Bloemfontein, accused of being unpatriotic.

'I even got into a fight with two officers of the Enniskillen Dragoons,
after suggesting we recompense the Zulus for our unlawful
invasion of their territory,
and defended the propriety of two loin-clad native women,
at the mercy of the licentious soldiery.'

'Oh,' answered her astounded companion,
'in that case you seem like the right chap for me,
for I'm now secretly working for Indian independence.'

'Let me introduce you to my mentor,
he models himself on John The Baptist,
the chap who prophesied the arrival of Jesus Christ.

'You can address him as Father of the Mahatma.'

A ripping yarn

'I say, it's Flinty!' Shouted 'Timmers', otherwise known as
Flying Officer Timothy Tamford-Tittimus,
his voice ringing round Mandevilles' Gentleman's Club,
where I, Flinty Flood-Flanners, was celebrating the 1918 Armistice.

I was relieved to see my pals hadn't noticed my embarrassment,
engrossed as they were in re-enacting the Eton Wall game.

You see, back in 1915 Tim had rescued me in his Royal Flying Corp plane,
the nearest I'd been to danger on what I thought was a 'cushy' posting.

Prone to blab after a few glasses of brandy,
I was concerned he might divulge the embarrassing nature of my mission.

Actually, back in those dark days of war, the strait-laced Timothy had
regarded me as some sort of boys-own hero.

He might have changed his tune however,
if he'd known my school nickname was 'Slinky',
due to my habit of peeking in French teacher Miss Pomdamolot's window,
who was forever standing in the moonlight, posing.

After a torrid meeting with the headmaster, sour-faced Dr Phillaprance,
I was expelled and, believing I would enjoy a privileged life,
joined my pater's old regiment, The King's Own.

But when war was declared we were off to France,
to suffer a right mauling at the Battle Of The Marne,
and I was soon begging the old man to pull some strings.

He obliged by securing me a desk job in Palestine, not from paternal love,
but because I was aware of his double life
(he used to smoke opium at his club, The Athenaeum).

Though Major Mungo McDougall gave me a hard time,
I got my revenge when he was lost in the desert and I came to his aid.

Only for the bad-tempered sod to receive a kick from my favourite camel,
Nasty Nero, to be then licked all over by his sister, Gutsy Gertrude.

My chum, reporter Miles Manningham, tried to use this in his *Times* column,
Titbits from The Middle East, but was told he'd lose his cushy number,
as it was well known that he 'batted for the other side'.

Like me, he didn't fit into the military world
(you may wonder why he was not in uniform).

Why, he carried so much shrapnel, if you shook him he'd rattle,
after he was wounded at Mersa Matrude.

'As long as you don't bat for the enemy,' I said, 'nobody cares.'

'Yes,' he concurred, 'but now I'll have to limit myself to reporting fashion blunders.'

'Any examples?' I asked. 'I could do with a laugh.'

'Well, I was in the officers' mess when that chap,
Lieutenant TE Lawrence turned up with a handsome W**g – sorry,
I meant native boy.

'Caused a stir, I can tell you, as TE was dressed like an Arab.
They'd come from Ackabar with news of a great victory,
achieved by crossing the desert, a route dismissed as impassable.

'Nevertheless, he and his raggedy band had won an almost bloodless battle.'

This was the first I'd heard of 'El Lawrens', as his followers called him,
I am of course referring to the enigma that was Lawrence Of Arabia,
a chap who became famous for his raids behind enemy lines.

Little did I know he'd identified me as a likely secret agent,
believing that nobody would suspect me, I being generally regarded as
'A nervous idiot, a chap who would jump when the clock chimes.'

He'd even enlisted the help of Bunty Bullens, the cousin
of his right-hand man, Freddie 'Fists' Fingleton.
Her and I would join glassy-eyed Arabs in a smoky-filled cellar,
where I became addicted to a deadly opioid.

Little did I know that, lost in my dope-filled languor, she'd marked me as blackmail material.

In other words, an addictive, lily-livered coward.

However, I was happy to avail of her supposed innocence,
knowing I was heading home where I was promised to Margaret,
daughter of Lord McOrkit-Mandale, rumoured to be as rich as Croesus,

I'd secured a return to England after telling the adjutant
that I'd noticed his visits to Madame Bumptious' back parlour.

Well, blackmail is one of the tools of a spy, isn't it?

I was celebrating in the mess only to be cornered by Lawrence,
who asked me to go behind enemy lines, emphasising there was no danger –
well, not much.

To which I replied, 'Thanks, but I'll have to opt out...'
only to hear the sinister words, 'I believe you know Miss Bunty...'

So that was his game – join me in my madcap lust for military honours,
where I'd likely meet my end at the hands of bloodthirsty Turks,
or I'll let a certain aristocrat back in Blighty know you've been consorting with a young lady.

I was at a loss as to what to do; should I disappear into the desert as a wandering hermit?

No, I'd probably get my throat cut.

How to get away from Fists was the problem.
I knew he frequented a card school and was in the habit of fixing the deck.
If only I could prove that, it could be my trump card, if you'll pardon the pun.

So, I followed him incognito to this den of iniquity, where a well-built female opium server seemed familiar.

Then her sleeve rolled up to reveal the emblem of my pater's regiment,
The King's Own.

Could it be him, surely not?

At my desk the next day I was trying to figure out this tangled web,
when in blundered a bent-over native cleaner, clanking a mop and bucket.

I barked at her, 'I say, I'm busy!'

Only for her to reply in a familiar voice, 'You always were an untidy pup!'

It was the pater, who blandly announced, 'Forgive me,
I'm a fan of Sherlock Holmes,
he was always startling doctor Watson by appearing in disguise.

'By the way, I've brought a friend to help you out of your predicament.'

Then in waltzed a young woman who immediately started to feel my thighs.
After catching my breath, I realised it was Miss Pomdampolot,
whom I'd last seen waving me off on the day of my expulsion.

'I watched you at games lessons when you scored lots of tries,' she said,
'and though you always scoffed lots of your English potato chips,
you were very fast.

'Anyway, we believe we can get you out of M,sieur Lawrens' silly mission.'

'Really, how?' I gasped.

'I blackmailed your very strait-laced headmaster,
who has connections at Whitehall, to get me a military posting.

'I knew him to be a secret society dilettante, calling himself Percy Philly-Pipps.

'I learned that mon Colonel 'Fightnot' McDougall, as we call him,
has asked headquarters if they have any useful rugby types
for the regimental rugby game,
as their best man has hurt himself riding a camel.'

'Oh,' I interjected, for I could see where this was heading, so explained,
'I was told by 'Kickalot' O'Toole, my school PT master,
that I was too small for rugby.'

'Oh, that old fool. I told him where to shove his ball, and even did,
when he became frisky.'

My father then added his two pennyworth, 'Now look here, young un,
I know you're a weakling, but you can, without taking up a rifle,
serve your king.

'Intelligence has learned that captain Montague Chastelady
is in the employ of one Mustapha Matingforce.

'This chap, a Turkish agent, is playing in the upcoming game,
and we suspect, as all the places he can hand over secrets are watched,
will use the match for that purpose.'

'Yes,' added his female assistant, 'we want you to tackle
Monty and steal the document,
before it can be handed to Mustapha, who will be there as a water carrier.'

'Steal it from where?'

She laughed, 'I assume it will be in his shorts.'

Looking embarrassed, the pater harrumphed, 'Standing by, after you limp
off with a feigned injury, will be Flying Officer Tamford-Tittimus,
to whizz you away in his plane.'

Which is why I was so embarrassed that day back in 1918,
to see that intrepid flyer Timmers.

But, many years later I'm now happy to embrace him,
for we've both been invited to mark the opening
of the new rugby stadium at Twickenham.

I shall reminisce about that infamous game in Palestine,
and reveal how I, an officer and a gentleman,
did the most ungentlemanly act of all,
pleading, 'Referee, I was only looking for the ball!'

A country walk

My lady friend and I set out for a walk in the beautiful Trough Of Bowland,
that hidden area popularised in verse by Stan Siddlesox,
the bard of Accrington, whose childhood was spent
in dreams of those distant peaks, as told in his biography,
From Cobbles to Stardom, and whose father, like mine,
is said to have exclaimed, 'Oh, dear wife, I love him dearly,
but by 'eck, we've reared an eccentric son!'

'I bet Stan's creativity wasn't stultified by those blasted pills,' I mused,
those herself makes me take – what are they called, metraline, sertraline?'

I thought of him as we neared those hills (which in previous centuries,
as he'd eulogised in his book, *Ode To Forgotten Lancashire Oaks*,
had boasted a huge forest, until it was felled to build
the ships that defeated Spain's armada) as we set off to walk up Totridge Fell,
a hill I'd run up as a Blackburn, Gateshead or Liverpool Harrier,
I can't remember which.

Anyway, like Tiger Woods, I had many clubs – athletic, that is.
Oh, those days were great fun, covered in mud, chasing
the leaders but never quite making the standard I felt I ought to.
Ah well, it was good for my mental health, and running is all the rage now.

Now I just walk in the park and watch the unfit struggle round
in that modern equivalent of the gym, the park run,
and shout, 'I was better than you!'

'But nobody listens', I thought, reflecting on those
former athletic days as, fortified with porridge as
per my diet – apparently it's good for the serotonin levels in my brain,
and the bowels (or is that All Bran?) – I huffed and puffed up the hill,
regretting the cake we'd enjoyed in the Barlick-Upon-The Vale village hall,
produced courtesy of Mrs Darcy-Dovecot.

'That lady,' I said to my gorgeous friend, 'looks like the
character from Charles Dickens' *Dombey And Son*, Mrs Bakealot.'

She looked puzzled, 'I don't remember her in that book.'

'Oh, I must be mistook.'

She looked at me quizzically, 'You're talking in rhyme.'

'Actually, we both are. Those pills you give me usually subdue it.'

But she pointed out, 'It was your doctor who recommended Sertraline.'

Well, the day went on in glorious colours and I encouraged her to sing,
and she obliged with Celtic classics *Molly Malone* and *Bogey's Bonnie's Belle.*

I applauded, then asked if she was Irish.
But she laughed, and dazzled my world with a huge smile.
'What, with my Jamaican accent?

'When I go in O'Halloran's bar I stand out like a sore thumb.'

'I'm sure they love you, just like wot I do.'

'Now don't be fresh, I'm on duty and expected to be professional.'

At the summit I looked to the east where the clouds massed over Weets Hill,
another distant prominence that I'd once ascended in string vest and shorts,
which, to my mind, looked so menacing, like a towering giant cat,
while its attendant cumuli resembled a cowering mouse.

I described my vision to herself, who laughed,
'You should paint your visions, they are so eclectic.'

'Alas,' I replied bitterly, 'I have no artistic skill,
but was – to quote the British Poetic Institute,
"*A writer who tries to distil his life through dubious imagery,*
which he has the effrontery to claim to be poetic."'

Herself commented, 'Well, you had lots of followers
on the poetry/live gig circuit,
but somehow your nerves got the better of you.'

'Ah, the nerves, I could give you chapters and verses about them,
all ending with n – rumination, obsession, depression, and finally compulsion,
but I don't feel compelled to, so I can strike the last one of the list.'

Then she gave me a kiss (just on the cheek, alas),
but I returned to the hospital enlivened by our day out,
and particularly her sexy smile, which filled me with its warmth,
as she let me unlace her boots, but alas I descended into the blues,
made worse 'cos I'd run out of decent books.

So I went in the TV room – only to last five minutes, for the others,
a lot of bores, were watching football,
with cliche-ridden commentary,

talking about 'Little triangles and a three-two-one formation',
or something like that.

I started ruminating, which in mental health jargon, means 'obsessive and intrusive thoughts'.

Well, BBC pundit Larry Linebreaker's banal remarks,
such as 'Wow, that was a good shot!' were really intruding upon me.
Besides, I thought, 'I could have scored that'.

So to break the cycle, I consulted Fred, a reformed alcoholic,

'Do you have to understand maths to watch this?'

His reply was succinct. 'No, just pissed.'

Then my mind slipped into reverse, as is its habit.
I remembered a know-it-all, who, when I was shy and gauche, had advised,
'You should cultivate popular things, to fit in, such as pop music and football.'

But I couldn't; you see I've always been odd.

I grew up reading Sherlock Holmes' creator Arthur Conan Doyle,
who attended a public school, coincidentally not far from Totridge fell,
and Rider Haggard, whose hero killed more African elephants than Hannibal,
but his readers never took him to task, for the slaughter of
so many beasts in pursuit of the elephant tusk.

I mused on this hypocrisy, then drifted into a dream I'd had as a kid,
where, as a big game hunter, just like Haggard's creation Alan Quatermain,
I fought off the rampaging Zulu, before retiring to my cottage at Capetown.

Now I escape into a world of boys-own stories
in my room at Wetherbeaten Hall,
an exclusive (a misnomer if ever there was one) psychiatric institute,
and dream up stories populated by my fictional heroes.

'But dash it Holmes!' Doctor Watson said, 'I can't remember what I wrote.
What was that one about the monster animal called?
The Cat Of The Whiskervilles?'

'Very funny!'

'Thanks!' Watson replied, 'I should have been a writer.'

'You were.' A voice interceded. 'Have you been taking your pills?'

The next morning my therapist reassured me, 'A problem aired is one shared.'

'Ah but,' I replied, 'as some woman once claimed,
I don't live in the real world.'

'Who told you that?' He asked.

'Probably the wife, when she put me in here.'

Then a door opened and a Jamaican voice said, 'No, it was me.'

'Do you mind!' The aggrieved medical chap shouted,
then looked at her closely. 'Didn't you retire, nurse Dreadlock?'

'Yes, and now I'm dispensing love, doctor Medilock,
instead of his daily pill.

'Just like the day I took him up, the beautiful Totridge fell.'

Then she held my hand. 'I'm not a nurse any more,
so will you marry me?

'Now that I don't have to be professional?'

Claire And The Flying Carpet

Claire decided to annoy her schoolteacher by swallowing a shoe,
then admitted afterwards that she'd felt a right heel,
'cos Miss Bluemantwit started to panic when Claire's face turned blue.

However, she was reassured by the naughty pupil,
who, in a muffled voice, said, 'Don't worry, it's only a trick!'

But before the other kids could call for help, out came the indigestible item
which turned into a magical carpet, upon which sat a little dog.

Claire then jumped on the carpet and flew away to Lanzarote,
to be met by the island's chief of police, who demanded to know,

'Why did you come here without obtaining a flying permit?
You nearly caused an upset with a jumbo jet by sneaking in under the fog,
and your animal should have a pet passport.'

She replied, 'Please Mr Policeman, I have fond memories of this island,
for it's where I was endowed with volcanic velocity.

'My dad took me up an extinct volcano, of which this island has many,
and being a curious child I collected a strange dust.

'Ever since then I've been able to do amazing feats.

'However, my powers are fading. So can you let me go?
Please, you really must!'

Unused to dealing with charming infants,
the inspector found himself agreeing to her request.

That morning a portly Englishman, Bulstrode Botheringman,
was conducting a naked mindfulness session,
when a carpet appeared in the sky.

'Watch out, hippies!' Came the cry, as Claire landed,
shielding her eyes, saying, 'I won't look!'

'Oh, don't worry luv, we're all respectable folk,'
Mr Botheringman assured her,
'I, for instance, am a retired school inspector.'

What happened next is unclear, but a story emerged about strange
events on the far side of the island.

It appeared to stem from a group of elderly New Age people,

who chanted, 'Where is our little Miss and her tiny dog,
who flew in one day then left us forlorn, watching as she sped off on her rug?'

Eager for a story, journalist Miles McMuttermuck tracked down a bitter,
drink-addled retired inspector of schools.

However, he soon decided the chap was fooling,
after he ranted about being ostracised by his fellow spiritualists,
over exaggerated stories of a carpet that was seen flying.

He asked, 'You're sure you were a school inspector?'

'Yes, I taught in London, but grew tired of the kids' antics.

I think they saw themselves as future Banksies,
always painting 'Up the 'Ammers', that's West Ham Football Club,
don't you know, on the toilet wall, instead of doing their arithmetic.'

Sensing he was losing the initiative, Miles asked, 'How did you get on with the girl?'

'Great, I encouraged her to go back to school, and take me with her on the carpet.'

The reporter nearly spilled his beer at this. 'You've seen it?'

'Of course, gave us all a right good scare, I don't mind telling you.
And...' he leaned closer, expelling lager fumes.

... 'I know she's become the focus for those weak-minded,
so-called spiritualists who see her as some sort of deity.'

'Really, do you know where she is, and will you take me there?'

'Indeed, for a small fee.'

'Of course, but you need to be sober.'

'Oh,' he answered defiantly, 'I'll be the model of sobriety.'

The next day the pair climbed an extinct volcano,
of which the island boasted many.

As Miles followed his guide, he wondered what he'd let himself in for,
but consoled himself that it would make a good piece to sell to a tabloid.

Then below he saw an assortment of naked people, practising yoga.
At which Bulstrode said, 'We're here.'

'I can see that,' his companion replied.
'What a weird sight, but I don't see a carpet.'

But he jumped as a shrill voice piped up, 'No, it's not weird, but cool.
As for the magical flying thing, I'm sitting on it.'

The startled pair looked round to see the rapscallion who started all this,
floating on something that one should really have been standing on.

'I didn't believe it when this chap told me about you,' Miles commented.

'How's it fly, does it have an engine?'

'No, it's magic,' Claire giggled, 'Do you want a lift?'

'What about the dog?'

'Oh, just tell him to shift.'

Botheringman shuffled back to town and his barstool.
'That was a nice little earner,' he said to himself,
'I'll just wait for the next idiot reporter to turn up.'

Then off that very coast a new island was discovered,
that was subsequently visited by an American scientific team.

But when the expedition leader, Max Middlepile,
got out his atmospherical testing machine, he cried,
'The sky is full of combustible sulphur.
All it needs is one spark.'

Then up piped a shrill voice, 'Don't worry, we can fly away on my carpet.'

Startled, Max and his fellow eggheads were amazed to see Claire.

'Am I seeing things!' He cried in panic.

'Don't worry, boss!' his assistant reassured him.
'It's the sulphur, it must be hallucinogenic.'
As they stared at a girl in mid air.

'Look, clever clogs,' she cried, 'I'm real and so are the flames below us.
And Fido's tail is wagging up and down.'

Max looked sceptical. 'What's odd about that?'

'It normally goes sideways, the inner core is upsetting her balance.'

Max sniffed, 'And her rear end.'

'No, that's the sulphuric acid, not flatulence.'

Max finally shook himself and said, 'You mean this island is volcanical?'

'Well, I don't think our geology teacher used that word in our class.
She talked about the earth's crust and teutonic plates.'

He laughed, 'Don't you mean tectonic?'

'Anyway, as you Americans say, we're between a rock and a hard place.
So, to use another Americanism, move your ass!'

Seconds later they were soaring above the waves,
swamping their previous, albeit only temporary residence.

'Heck,' lamented Max, 'I was about to name it Middlepile's Isle.'

'That's a good name, my English teacher, Miss Honora Hunstanton,
would be impressed, as she likes names that alliterate.'

'Ah, I can see it's easy to impress you, but alas, not so my fiancée,
Miss Happensteate, of Washington Watermeadows, Wisconsin.

She challenged me to do something incredible, or she wouldn't wed me.'

'Doesn't sound like a nice girl.'

'She's lovely, but like many of the privileged fairer sex needs
something to show off about. '

'You're old fashioned, Max. Like my teacher, Miss Bluemantwit.
You two would make a good fit.'

At this point a storm blew in from the Sahara desert,
and my Central Intelligence Agency tracker device went on the blink.

You see, dear reader, I Hank Hunter, secret agent,
had been following the adventures of this remarkable girl
(I know this must have come a surprise, but I am a spy after all)
hoping to harness the power of her amazing carpet.

I contacted agents throughout the Mediterranean, and was briefly sidetracked
by a report of an unidentifiable flying object over the Balearics,
those islands that, like Lanzarote, are dominions of Spain.

My colleague, Horace Horselicks, then followed up a lead gained in a
Majorcan nightclub from Señorita Fernandez.

However, being rather piddled, his CIA accent-locating antennae
failed to notice that she dropped her aitches, as in 'Up the 'Ammers',
a sign that her accent originated from the London district of West Ham.

Her tip off led him to a mountain village in the belief he'd found
what the US government was looking for,
only to be set upon by several roustabouts.

On overcoming them with karate punches and kicks,
they told him, 'Calm down, señor, you have a mighty fist.
We were sent to rob you by a Señor Botheringham.

'That woman you met in the Pensive Parrot club is his daughter.'

But despite staking out the aforementioned establishment,
the trail had gone cold,
and we could find no trace of little Claire and her airborne carpet.

Then a strange article appeared in *The Times.*

WEIRD EVENTS ON SPANISH ISLAND
Reports of levitation in Lanzarote and disappearing
scientists have been linked to an English girls school,
writes MILES McMUTTERMUCK

*'Miss Darcy-Dropstool, Headmistress of the
Montmorency College For Young Ladies,
in the English village of Much-Swithinthwaite,
told police that one of her most reliable teachers, Miss Bluemantwit,
had claimed that one of her pupils had flown away on a carpet.*

*The lady, a known spinster, then announced her engagement to someone
whom she laughingly said 'possessed an equally daft name!'*

*The two disappeared after the service, and it is believed that
their sudden departure is linked to the arrival of an irate American woman,
Miss Happensteate.*

*Research revealed that the newly-weds set up a scientific
establishment on the island of Lanzarote,
where they are attempting to harness the power of an extinct volcano.*

*Following information gained from a Mr Bulstrode Botheringman,
I penetrated the inner region of the aforementioned island, then,
climbing a rocky slope, was knocked over by a little dog.*

*I got up, dazed, to hear a shrill English voice calling, '
Come back Fido!'
then out of an impenetrable fog appeared a young girl,*

who announced, 'We'll take him to meet Miss Bluemantwit.
She likes meeting the curious who visit our little isle.'

Alas, patient readers of my column,
I don't remember what happened
after my encounter with the mist-shrouded canine.

All I'll say is that I was found wandering, apparently drunk,
and taken into police custody, pending payment of a fine.

I'm now waiting for my editor to contact the
embassy and arrange my release.'

So the mystery continues.
You may wonder what happened to me, Hank Hunter,
once regarded as the Central Intelligence Agency's sharpest operator.

Well, after my failed mission and subsequent disgrace,
I retired to Lanzarote to run a bookshop.

Well, you never know, that elusive Little Claire might fly in,
on the carpet!

Claribella Constance

As I gazed around that vast music hall, The Palladium,
I wished a fervent 'Good luck!' to my favourite singer,
Miss Claribella Constance, and was rewarded with a wave
from behind the stage curtain.

I remembered when, as a young girl, a roving gypsy, Ma McDonogool,
prophesied, 'Her heart is full of high notes, yet I sense there is unfulfilled
passion.'

As a teenager I thought I was in there! until I received a punch in the solar
plexus.

I should have remembered she was St Swithins School boxing champion,
and had a neat right hook, when I enticed her to share a bottle of cider and then
tried for a kiss.

However, keen to impress my mates, I took it as an opportunity to boast
But my indiscretion and her tempestuous nature set
her on a torturous path out of our village, leaving me pitifully forlorn.

For when farmer Smithins, eager to add her to the list adorning his bedpost,
sought her maidenhead on a frosty night, after promising a ride on his horse,
she kicked him in the Donegals, shouting, 'You're not adding me to your
conquests!'

'I'm an artist,' she shouted, 'and what's more can sing like a fog horn,'
and she did, then stole his trusty steed Run Like The Wind,
who laughed and pranced at his newfound freedom.

My love remaining unrequited, and hearing tales of
an operatic rider in wayside villages,
I tracked her to Nottingham where I learned she'd
established a reputation as a warbling waitress in a Robin Hood theme bar,
with Run Like The Wind giving kids dressed as peasants rides in Sherwood
Forest.

Alas, her heart broken by a bow and arrow salesman, she left,
after sobbing her heart out to a very camp Jodhpur Japes,
a retired actor who recited a mediaeval ballad about Tam Lin,
that lustful knight who enticed young maidens with wine-sodden grapes.

‘Alas, dear girl,’ he told her, ‘your lover has gone to flog his wares
to Viking reenactors in Denmark and Finland.

‘You, I’m afraid, are a victim of male hetero dominance.’

Intrigued, she asked, ‘What’s that?’

‘Well, it’s a term coined by a radical thinker who is making a name for himself.’

‘Oh, what’s he called?’

‘Alas, my memory fails me, but I hear he’s been described as ‘magical’,
and helps young women find their artistic self.

‘He’s seeking converts to his rebellious commune above the city of Brighton.’

So off Claribella rode to arrive in the gay resort,
arriving with a smile for the milkman who, impressed by her speedy steed,
added this feisty female to his list of people to know,
promising to help her find this ‘magical’ man,
in the seaside town where the ‘queer’ men and women go.

So, in return for racing Run Like The Wind along The Downs for bets,
Claribella was directed to a cavern, the home of latter-day hippies,
who were enveloped in a fog of cannabis.

Feeling she’d been sent on a wild goose chase, she was about to go,
but bumped into Magical Malcolm, whose eyes opened with
delight when she declared,
‘I’m desperately trying to discover my inner self.’

So he took her to Harlot’s Hill, and announced,
‘This is where neolithic man practised fertility rites.

‘I take all my female followers here, by way of an initiation,’
and he made his fateful move, only like me before him,
to fall victim to Claribella’s boxing skill.

She showed him a neat side step, followed by a quick one-two,
and was only stopped from inflicting serious hurt by a policeman who emerged from the bushes.

‘No need for fisticuffs,’ declared the sergeant, ‘just let me read him his rights.’

‘Oh,’ she laughed, ‘as long as they’re not the ones he was referring to.’

‘Good on yer lass,’ came a cry from a babel of young women.

‘We knew what he was up to Claribella,
so we thought we’d save your blushes,’
they declared, as Malcolm was taken to the police station.

You may wonder where I was in all this fuss.
Well, knowing of her interest in art, on arrival in the
famous resort I sought out arty types,
and among these was art tutor Marcus Mansett,
who asked me to model for his class.

I turned up and stripped, only to hear an audible gasp,
blinking in amazement at you-know-who, sitting there with an easel.

She informed me she’d been making ends meet by singing
and sketching on the pier,
with her pals from the cave as backing singers,
cashing in on her reputation as
the girl who brought down a notorious cult leader.

Always keen for a bargain, I took her to that popular eatery,
HP Featherflumes, taking advantage of their two-for-one offer.

But after chiding me for being a cheapskate,
she ended up in the arms of ‘Big’ Bud Coyote,
a millionaire cowboy who’d bought one of her paintings,
of a whale stranded on a pebble-strewn beach beneath a chalk cliff,
which she claimed was, ‘Symptomatic of my life,
stranded among a rock and a hard place’,
and she was soon adorning the old homestead he’d built on the Downs,
to replicate his childhood home, Forever Windblown.

At first their love blossomed; Bud even raced Run Like The Wind
in the County Coastal Chase, bagging a 100 guineas,
and she attended social events with him as he bought up half of Sussex.

Undeterred, I followed along in his wake, a pitiful besotted creature.

However, Claribella thrilled with delight when I was allowed to
accompany her to opera venue Glyndebourne, after Coyote had declared,
‘I’d rather listen to the shrieking Indians I watched in

Wild Bill Hiccup's Wild West Circus,
than those strutting divas – besides, they aren't a patch on Dolly Parton.'

It was when the couple visited the US that discordant notes were heard,
after Claribella wanted to visit the valley of the Little Big Horn,
where Chief Crazy horse defeated General Custer,
in a battle over the sacred Sioux Indian lands in the Black Hills Of Dakota.

'Why are you so interested in that?' Coyote asked her angrily.

'I was a tomboy,' she answered, 'and read about the Wild West and its Indians,
in particular how children were slaughtered at the valley of the Washita,
by Custer and his regiment.'

An enquiring journalist, hearing about this interesting visitor from Brighton,
asked her, 'Have you met The Queen?'

'I did in Brighton,' she laughed, 'but not the one you mean.'

Advertisers cashed in on her fame, and she was pictured on a horse,
opening a cowboy convention, wearing a low-cut bodice singing a
country hit that was all the rage.

Broadcast live, this publicity got record numbers tuning into the radio waves.
She sang, 'I fell in love with a cowboy from Leningrad,
who told me he was a clown with the Soviet State Circus,'
with the chorus, 'But now I'm all alone and sad,
after he left me for a Cossack from Moscow called Boris.'

Then she suddenly disappeared, but was spotted swimming and singing,
sans-clothes in a remote bay off the Irish coast,
with a Dolphin she nicknamed Dolores, who was feeling seasick.

Claribella believed the animal was suffering from anxiety,
after hordes of tourists flocked to see her swimming in the Atlantic.

However, the publicity about 'A naked hussy whose lewd behaviour has
brought hosts of nudists to the Emerald Isle,
and dealt a blow to tourism by luring a popular marine animal to her bosom',
made her furious.

So she enlisted the help of the Taoiseach (Irish Prime Minister),
who raised the matter in the Dáil,
resulting in the establishment of a school for dolphins,

where they were given therapy and sent back out to splash
and entertain the curious.

Well, that is a brief resume of my sweetheart's career up to this moment,
as she prepares to face a packed London Palladium.

As I ruminated on the journey which had taken her thus far,
I saw some familiar names – Farmer Smithins and
Magical Malcolm – out on bail – then as the lights went down,
in sneaked a glowering Bud Coyote,
making a racket in spurs and Stetson.

On she came to thunderous applause, saying,
'I would like to dedicate this number to my boyhood friend,
and she pointed at me, 'who, being a lusty sod,
propelled me on a journey which led to this place'.'

At this everyone stared at me, in particular those rascally types
I alluded to above.

But she laughed, and said, 'See you later darling.
Oh, and I owe you a kiss.'

My lost love of Hicklegate

I sat in a quaint pub, guzzling its real ales,
and wondering how I could reconnect with Gabriela,
my lost love, who was somewhere in Hicklegate,
that famous spa town of North Yorkshire.

Then, staggering past the war memorial,
I was halted in my tracks by a preacher, and stood transfixed
as he told me that 'Jesus saves'.

'Really?' I said to myself, thinking that this town attracts some right oddballs,
while noting that the evangelical orator was
from a nearby secret establishment,
up there in the hills, rumoured to be a listening post
for the post Cold-War era.

This military base, used by our American cousins to guard our shores,
is, due to its design, known locally as the 'Golf Balls'.

Ordered by PC Middlehump to partake of a strong coffee,
or face a sojourn in the cells, I encountered Miss Theresa Thistlebinhire,
a visiting writer from the Canadian town of Montmorency Falls.

'I'm paying homage to author Agatha Christie,'
she declared, 'who fled to that hotel behind us,
hoping to stay incognito,
in an effort to escape from an adulterous husband.'

We got on so well that I offered to be her guide,
but my tourist talk was interrupted by a drifter called
'Bebop' Brian, swaying to a tune booming from the
radio held tightly in his fist.

Then Theresa invited him to The Nosy Novelist,
a Waterspoons hostelry, for fish and chips.
We left him snoozing behind a plant plot and escaped
to Hicklegate's famous cafe Parlour, Buncies,
for tea and an expensive cake.

Outside, a busker called Singing Sam gave us
Procol Harum's *A Whiter Shade of Pale*, then asked,
'Have you any requests?

'I've a great playlist, ranging from prog rock to skiffle,
and do a great version of *My Old Man's a Dustman.*'

Prompting me to remark, 'You look like you've been sleeping in one.'

But his response cut me to the quick,
'You'll be in one if you don't stop drinking so much ale.'

Then I asked Theresa, 'Has your research revealed
that Dracula dined in that establishment you've just left?'

She looked surprised, 'Really?'

But the annoying busking man interjected, 'Did he have tea and stake?'

Theresa laughed, adding, 'Maybe he came here after
landing in Whitby, in a ship full of the dead.'

Some mischievous spirit compelled me to add,
'Indeed, the count called the manager of Buncies a bloodsucker,
after complaining about the prices.'

Just then my lost love appeared, escorted by an American military type,
who introduced himself as Loo-tenant Bugs Brooksplately,
explaining, 'I do something with cyphers.'

The military chap announced, 'I have an affinity with this town,
due to my grandad Fred.

'He came here, after the Battle of Ypres, pronounced Wypers.

'Let me introduce you to this lovely lady, a Ukrainian refugee,
whom I've made most welcome, inspired by our Saviour Jesus.'

'I bet you did,' I thought.

Jealous of this fellow, I could only hide my chagrin,
as he told Theresa how his grandfather had danced with Agatha Christie,
while she was holed up in his hotel, confessing to fleeing the front line,
a shell-shocked wreck.

But being a trained actor, had reinvented himself
as an artist on Paris' Left Bank, calling himself Monsieur Magleflat.

Then Bebop Brian popped up again, saying he's forming a
band with our busking pal, called The Drifters.

'That name's already been taken,' I pointed out.

'Aye, he agreed, 'But they're a black foursome,
while we're a duo, and white.'

'Let's celebrate,' Theresa said, 'by all going for fish and chips,
in the Nosy Novelist, my treat.'

Arriving in said place, Gabriela sat under a portrait of Agatha Christie,
while I sneakily joined her, putting Bugs' nose out.

She nodded at the artistic work, saying, 'That's by Bugs' grandad,
he was a refugee of sorts, fleeing war, like me.'

Then to my dismay she blandly announced, 'I'm now a Christian,
devoted to the sect with the great title of We're All Born Again,
founded by Loo-tenant Bugs Brookplately,
so I shall not partake of alcohol.

'But if you think I want his hand in marriage,
cute though he is, you are a fool!'

So ended a day which began with me as 'A drunken disgrace',
according to a policeman, and ended a reunion with my sweetheart,
thanks to an American who works in a 'golf ball'.

He's no doubt able to hear my new-found love say,
'I love it in Hicklegate.

'I've found a new friend called Theresa,
who is just one in a long line of oddballs.'

By which you'll gather that the Canadian has said goodbye
to her birthplace of Montmorency Falls.
For a genius is never appreciated in his, or her own country.

But herself, Bebop Brian and Singing Sam, find it ironic that
finding my lost love has now condemned me to a life of sobriety!

Miss Coffee drinker

I wonder, Miss Coffee 'Suppa', what do you think of
when sipping your daily brew, as you sit like a cute mouse?

Your ears a-twitch to a variety of accents, from Geordie,
in the north east of England, with its castle that's always new,
or that shrill sound emanating from our most musical city of Mersey land –
Scouse.

You know, where that 'musical combo' came from, the one named after a type
of insect?

Be of good cheer and swing that crazy golf club, in the gardens of dahlias,
delphiniums and drooping fronds, then sniff those alluring scents.

Remember the good times in that county of mountains and tarns,
still making up story-book adventures (at your age indeed!).

Of teenage escapades in South Sea oceans, discovering lost treasure,
coral hunting and nearly getting the 'bends', oh, what great yarns!

Or the Pondlife series, about swimming rats, submarinal puppies off their lead,
and endangered newts in murky ponds.

We will talk of watery monsters, little lambs carolling by Bolting Beck,
and my inability to have a smooth forty winks.

Do you really miss those television stars, Loose Ladies and Phantom Deck?
For deep down you're more than a bored former wife,
obsessively telly watching.

Maybe we could have a chat, and lament your exclusion from
did-you-see that-programme-on-the-box gossiping – I know a hostelry
which serves limitless hot drinks.

Then to my surprise Miss Coffee Lover popped up, would you believe it,
In that very pub, behind a palm in the beer garden?

She said, ‘I’m checking this plant for Green Fingered Fungus’.

‘I was a gardener, back in the Canadian town of Mannatudemungus,
where I was married to a Canadian Mounted Policeman.

‘Alas, he put me on a horse against my wishes,
and I got a sore rear end,
due to that rather handsome, but controlling cop.

‘So we went dancing at the village ceilidh,
where I became a disgruntled cop’s missus,
for all he would do was drink beer and glumly clap.

‘Disillusioned by love, he rode off into the sunset with a right slapper,
who couldn’t even dance.’

‘I left Mannatudemungus disguised as a tinker,
sneaking out at night in a horse and cart.

‘So I’ll be brave and say hello, and though we’ve met by chance,
I believe it was down to fate.

‘But before we start, please tell me you don’t like horse riding,
and won’t be a pain in the a**se?’

Hello Mammy, you've found me!

I ran 5,000 metres on a running track in 14 minutes and 34 seconds,
a personal best by a country mile, but I didn't really enjoy
the cut and thrust of track and field, preferring those 'medium' fell
races where I could race down a gradual descent,
leaping like a stag over rock and stile.

For I liked to pretend I could mix it with the 'tough men of the fells',
and pick up easy prizes.

Which is what I did the day I raced over Stoodley Pike.

Afterwards, having missed out on a first prize due to my lack
of strength on the climb,
an old Gypsy woman stood watching me put on my trousers.

She declared, 'Ah, you took the easy option, when you should have been at
the open track and field meeting, doing the 3,000metres.

'You should concentrate on lowering your middle-distance times.

'Why, your coach always said you had no discipline.
Which is true, and, desiring a better life than I could provide in my caravan,
you left Erin's Isle for the shores of Albion.

'But now, as the chief attraction of Murgatroyd's Travelling Fair,
fate has led me to West Yorkshire's Pennines.

'I've followed your athletic progress with interest,
and you can't half shift, like a startled hare.'

Looking at me, her smile fading, she prophesied,
'There will come a time when you're no longer as fit as a butcher's dog,
and will enter a seedy world far from these shores,
like a Victorian criminal in those novels you liked to read,
hugging the London smog.'

'In years to come you will blossom, as a chatter-up of women,
but your old pals will categorise you as another in their long list of mighty
bores.

'But beware a scantily-clad femme fatale clad in cut-price bling.'

A fellow athlete said to me, 'Was that your mum?'

'Gawd, no!' I expostulated, embarrassed.

'She's a 'Gyppo' woman.'

Many years later I thought of this prophecy while lounging in a Florida hotel,
a favourite haunt of movie moguls, aged porn stars and plastic surgeons,
a refuge for the makers of fakery, and started to cry.

The wife asked, jingling her cheap sparklers,
which she wore even while in a bikini,
'What's the matter, darling?'

'I've got all that a man desires,' I sobbed, 'but I'm old and fat,
and can no longer run up and down that pike called Stoodley.

'But in those days I was competing with genuine people,
and I left my heart on a Yorkshire hill.

'Now I realise there's more to life than sun lounging
with an old Hollywood flop,
who looks ridiculous in a bikini.

'So, drink up and move out, you've had your fill!'

Then she slapped me very hard, spilling her Martini.

But I bravely continued, 'I've been living a lie – for instance,
remember the couple I introduced as my parents at our
wedding in the Hollywood hills?

'Well, they were masquerading at my expense.

'A music hall act, known as Pop up Percy and Disappearing Polly,
they dazzled with sleight of hand, but come quite cheap,
if you booked them with a band.'

My lounging marital partner looked surprised,
'Oh them, they're on stage here tonight.'

'Are they? Oh, what a coincidence.

'Well, Percy had a reputation as a pickpocket,
which got him a bad name on the cabaret circuit.

'Indeed, some witty scribe writing in the *Magician's Monthly* referred
to them as Polly And Percy Hides The Disappearing Pence.

'Which was ironic as, looking back at the first stanza,
you'll know my early life, like theirs, was also marked by pretence.

'So, you're a fraud!' The irate missus shouted.
'writing scripts for naughty skin flicks.'

'Yes,' I countered, 'back in those non-PC days.'

'I based them on those tales you told me of your early movie roles.'

'Well,' she screamed, 'Your scripts were full of posh ladies wearing corsets
and stays.'

'And you're a snob,' I countered, 'known as the diva of hotel swimming pools.

'Like now, showing your wealth off in this exclusive hotel in Miami.'

Then onto the poolside came an old woman, and I trembled with shock,
recalling the day of my birth when the nurse had slapped my bottom.

Years later I felt life was coming full circle as I legged it down a hill,
as poor as a church mouse, for that bleeding Percy had picked my pocket.

I hid as the old woman walked over to my startled wife, saying,
'Hello, I'm his mammy.'

Malachi Middlemound

As a rugby league fan, there are many tales I relish of the great game,
but none are as remarkable as that of the little lad who ignored
the critics to fulfil his lifelong dream.

In a northern city not too long ago, Malachi Middlemound,
all five-foot two of him, harboured a secret ambition – to
play rugby for his hometown.

But notorious braggart, 'Bruiser' Bill Billycan,
would laugh, saying 'What, you?'

So he would escape from the world with his pet pigeon Sally,
hoping like her, he too could fly away from life's woes.

Instead, he read tales of adventure by
H Rider Haggard and Rudyard Kipling,
imagining he was a big game hunter,
stalking a tiger or fighting that mighty warrior nation, the Zulu.

The shy boy would wave at rugby star, Barrie McDomittas,
one of his sporting heroes,
whom the matchday presenter would introduce as,
'He's big and he's bad'.

Then one day 'Big Baz' told him, 'Get down to the Lock Lane club
and play the toughest sport of all, young fellah me lad.'

Inspired, he was soon running around with an oval ball,
dreaming of streaking up the pitch,
like a leopard on the African Savannah.

But one day his friend Septimus found him looking forlorn,
so asked, 'What's the matter, old fruit, why are you looking so sad?'
(He liked to adopt an aristocratic voice, being a great fan of the
famed English humourist, PG Wodehouse).

'Lost your pocket money, or is Suzie Sillymot
still rejecting your advances?

'Cheer up, you're too young to be in love.'

But Malachi looked up in tears, 'No, none of the above.
My PE teacher says I'm too small to play rugby.'

‘Come to the prayer meeting,’ his Methodist pal advised,
‘and you will find meaning in all this.’

Once there he was filled with the spirit of evangelism,
as *Bible* in hand, he extolled the virtues of sobriety,
but felt like a fool when he condemned his beer-drinking flock,
for he knew that his dad,
according to the landlord of the Flying Ferret,
could ‘Drink it out of a sweaty sock’.

Then fate struck again when he met an ailing Doddie Weir.
Struck down by motor neurone disease,
he’d towered above the opposition as the tallest rugby union player,
leaping like a salmon to catch a line-out throw.

The legendary Scotsman said,
‘You’re not too small – take my fellow sufferer,
nicknamed The Pocket Rocket, Leeds’ lad Rob Burrow.

‘He’s so small you could put him in your pocket,’ he said with a laugh,
‘Did you know BBC commentator Bill McLaren
called me ‘The Galloping Giraffe?

‘Anyway, where was I? Oh yes... believe me, it’s not all about size.

‘Oh, Rob’s such a character, we could have had a double act,
just like Morecambe And Wise,
with me poking fun at Rob’s lack of height.

‘But my God he could shift, like a starling in flight,
lighting up a stadium with his darting runs,
just like I did when I became a British and Irish Lion.

‘We played hard and had fun, and behaved like fools.
Not like today’s lot, with their no-beer rules
and training-schedule pie charts.’

The little chap face brightened at these
words from a player beloved by all,
even those men in suits at Twickenham,
christened by Will Carling as ‘Old farts’.

Not too long after that Bill Billycan,
who’d once mocked a boy’s sporting desire,
was watching Leeds take on Castleford at his local, The Silvery Swan,

when the TV presenter, the now retired Barrie McDomittas,
announced, 'Watch out for my old team's debutant,
Malachi Middlemound.

'His coach says they have to wait before training for him to say a prayer,
but he's quick as lightning… hang on, he looks vaguely familiar…'

Well, if you loved watching Malachi play, read his biography,
***Never Give Up**, that year's best selling sports book.*
It's dedicated to Robert Geoffrey Burrow,
every little sporting kid's hero.
For just like Malachi, when Little Rob got the ball,
the fans roared so hard the old stand at Leeds shook.

Fall of a self-important prig

My name is 'Buncie' Billington-Brig, a genuine self-important old fool,
who loves to pontificate on society's ills while propping
up the bar in my local, The Dancing Duck.

I was happy in my pomposity, as befitting a secretary of the Masonic Hall,
until the night subtle hints were made that my wife – chairwoman of our
village branch of The Keep Britain Pure society, was anything but.

Indeed, one laughed and said, 'Pure she is not!',

Well, I'm afraid to say I rather over imbibed,
and was stopped by PC Cuffington.

He didn't succumb to my barely disguised attempt at bribery,
and I was duly up before the magistrate, an old school chum no less,
who got his revenge on a chap he remembered as the school bully.

So, forced to use Shanks's pony, I took to reflecting on all those
pompous Billington-Brigs who'd gone before me.

One, a boyhood hero, Colonel Jeremiah Gerontius,
had the honour to serve as an intelligence officer under General Gordon,
but managed to be elsewhere when that legendary military man
met his violent demise.

He'd claimed to be on an intelligence mission,
but Private McPherson knew different,
for, when the populace had slaughtered 'Gordon, hero of Khartoum',
Major Gerontius was hiding in a brothel along with the adjutant and regimental
physician.

But when faced with this, Jeremiah had simply said,
'How did he know it was me, for as a secret agent I
would have been in disguise?'

As a boy my head was filled with tales of this distinguished soldier,
but now I began to feel twinges of unease.

One day I met Reverend Tickle-Treats, who found me looking
at a stone in the church cemetery,
bearing the name of my family's distinguished campaigner.

'You know he was a fraud,' the cleric commented, 'your ancestral hero?'

I laughed, 'It wouldn't surprise me!'

The cleric nodded sagely, saying, 'But religions have their share of hypocrites.

'Take myself, whom my parishioners regard as a scion of moral values,
but unknown to them I'm actually a master criminal,
with dark deeds to my name.

'My ability to con, dissemble and cheat is unsurpassed,
according to Inspector Dallymoat of the French police.

'Born into a theatrical family I learned the skills of acting and make up,
but an inability to resist a pretty face saw me bring the family into disrepute.

'So, I took on a new persona, thanks to a Dr Fiddlefixit,
whose unethical medical practices made him a prime target for blackmail,
but conveniently for me is a plastic surgeon on
London's exclusive Harley Street,
and I'm now wanted on three continents by Interpol.'

I stood astounded thinking, 'And I thought I could pull the
wool over gullible eyes.'

'But there may be hope for you yet,' he continued,

'Indeed, he has been employed by law enforcement agencies.

'A psychologist has come up with a new reality TV show,
called Find the Fraud.

'He says I gave him the idea, for he is an expert in
examining facial expressions,
and saw through my attempts to enlist him in one of my dodgy schemes,

using a little-known technique called Fakefinds,
pioneered by Sigmund Freud.

'Anyway, what I mean is, they're looking for chaps just like you.'

I brightened up at this, and asked, 'Can my wife come?

'For she's not, as her social media post claims, 'as pure as the driven snow'.'

'I can confirm that,' the vicar astounded me by saying,
'I got to know her very well while you were banged up in the police station.'

'But she couldn't keep her mouth shut, and, expecting to be defrocked,
I'm now heading for Harley Street and an appointment
with my old pal, the plastic surgeon.'

You may wander what has become of me after this revelation – well,
I appeared on the aforementioned TV series, but didn't last long,
for I'd lost my love of being a pompous twit.

But if you visit The Dancing Duck you'll see my
former missus with her new husband, the Reverend Littlelove,
rocking with mirth as the regulars recall the night
her previous husband's pompous behaviour came unstuck.

She wouldn't have been so cheerful if she'd known who he really was.

For as you may have guessed, I persuaded the naughty cleric's
Harley Street pal to fashion me a new face.

After wooing my unsuspecting former adulterous missus,
we were soon walking down the aisle, cheered by PC Cuffington,
who didn't recognise me as the speeding pompous twit
he'd once put the cuffs on,
thus hastening my spectacular fall from grace.

A self-important twit I may have been, yet wasn't a patch on the chap whose
confession that day in the graveyard led me to emulate him,
and become a mighty fraud.

I speak of the village vicar, and I echo his parting words,
'Vengeance will be mine, sayeth the Lord.'

A marvellous mermaid

I strolled along the Dingle, taking a break from teaching
my psychology students, who'd scoffed when I'd claimed,
'Though I am of a logical bent,
I believe that there's more to this world than you think.'

When who should I meet but a marvellous mermaid,
sunning herself in the morning mist, quite an achievement in itself.
Among the riverside detritus, she shone like a beacon in the night.

This mythical creature seemed heaven sent,
especially when she sang my favourite Irish song,
*Dublin in the rare old time*s.

'I have just swum over from that very city,' announced this denizen of the sea,
'for we all know Liverpool is the real capital of Ireland.'

'Indeed,' I concurred, 'and you will light up its grim environs.
Indeed, my heart is already lighter, upon meeting you on Dingle Strand.'

'Thank you,' she replied, 'I'm told that most men like their
woman to have a nice bottom...'
and she leapt onto the harbour wall, 'but being a mermaid,
I don't have one.

'Maybe that's why I'm still single.'

My curiosity was piqued, 'Doesn't Cupid's arrow find
many targets among marine life?'

'Oh no, we do breed, for continuing the species is
more important than being, what you humans call 'a wife'.

'I did have a fling with an octopus who was great at foreplay,
and our lovemaking was truly adventurous.

'You could say his tentacles spread far and wide,
but I dumped him because he had awful flatulence.'

'Really? Too many mussels?'

'No, he loved seaweed and due to climate change, there's less of it.

'So, we came to Liverpool 'cos we heard it's great for weed,
but we were stranded by the tide.'

'Well,' I replied, 'the tide will turn in its own good time.'

'It can keep turning as far as Ossie is concerned,
'cos he's stoned out of his mind.'

'Ah, the wrong sort of weed?

'Well, his loss could be my gain.'

At which she gave me a sly smile, and I dared to risk a complement.

'You have a lovely smile, in fact it's your best feature.'

Laughing, she replied, 'You mean I don't have a big bust,
beloved of those misogynistic weavers of fairy tales, who,
when I applied to be a mythical sea creature,
wasn't given much of a chance.'

Amused, I asked, 'Oh, you're a feminist?

'Ah, she exclaimed, 'thereby hangs a tail.

I looked sceptical, 'Isn't it a fin...?'

'It's a tail composed of fins, according to my uncle,
Professor Smith of the Institute for Marine Biology.'

'Oh, I didn't realise mermaids were accepted by science.'

'Indeed not, and he has suffered the slings and arrows of you-know-what,
because of it.

'He deserves to be recognised by the scientific press,
whose attitude forced that other mythical favourite,
Nessie, to become a hermit.'

I laughed, 'I wondered why the Loch Ness Monster
had disappeared off the news.

'I thought it had been proven as a hoax.'

She laughed, 'Oh, you are a fool.'

Chastened, I replied, 'Thanks, people used to shout Nessie!
whenever they saw anything on the loch that floats.'

She snorted with derision, 'Yes, well I know she exists
and her disappearance is due to too much plastic,
which gives her terrible indigestion.'

'Oh!' I exclaimed, about to interrupt.

'So, she's gone to Glendalough in Ireland via a subterranean tunnel,
and suns herself above the upper lake in the cave formerly
inhabited by St Kevin.'

'Very funny.'

'No, I'm not jesting.'

'Oh, I suppose she's dating Finn McCool, Ireland's mythical giant.'

At this she turned her back on me, saying, 'You're taking the...'

'Oh, I'm sorry, it's just that I'm a man of science,
I've had enough of women of a logical bent,
being a professor of psychology.

'I was besieged by fortune hunters, since I won the Gilbertian cash prize for Inward Paths of Logic.'

'Did any of them access your fortune?'

'No, I discovered most of them turned out to be femme fatales.

'A mythical sea creature like you would be heaven sent – do you fancy a drink?'

She laughed, 'Okay, we'll go to The Slippery Eel, it's a great pub.'

My day continued its bizarre twist when she introduced me to some of her pals.

There was Ossie The Octopus, Cuthbert The Crab and Wally The Walrus, who sang a song to the tune of *Scarborough Fair.*

I met a mermaid who looked so pretty,
I tried a kiss but she poked me in the eye with her tail,
so I had to wear spectacles but lost them in a gale.

Chorus
Watch out for the marvellous mermaid who suns herself on the shore,
if you fall for her wiles, you'll sail never more.

So, take heed from a stricken sailor who fell foul of a mermaid's beauty.
Her flying tail left me looking for an optician, and I resolved to ignore
the charms of a fabled sea creature, and spend my time fishing.

Refrain
Watch out for the marvellous mermaid who suns herself on the shore,
if you fall for her charm, you'll be chastised by the bosun,
and sail never more.

I clapped loudly, commenting, 'He has a deep profundo bass, like the great singer Paul Robeson, famous for *Old Man River*, from the opera *Porgy and Bess*.'

'Indeed,' she agreed. 'He was black, wasn't he?

'And vilified for his ethnicity, just like us sea people.'

I looked sharply at her, 'Are mermaids ethnic?'

'Well, we are an endangered species.

'We need protecting, like the old and feeble.'

She then showed she was anything but, by slapping
her tail on the floor while Wally sang,
I fell in love with a dolphin, whose idea of love was
to tickle me with his snout.

'I only do fondling,' I cried, 'so keep your hands to yourself,
you big fat Walrus,
and if you don't stop drinking ale, you'll get gout!'

'So, I joined a dating site in the hope of attracting a partner, saying,
'If you want a big curvy mammal, I cruise in the English Channel.

'I drink seaweed wine and eat haddock, so I'm a cheap date.
So here I am still cruising, so I wish you all good night.'

I woke up on the beach at the Dingle with a start,
and tossed aside a joint of weed I'd been smoking,
then hummed a sea shanty I'd learned as a kid,

It was a Friday morn when we set sail,
and were not far from the land
when our captain, he spied a fishy mermaid with a comb
and a glass in her hand...

And I strolled home to finish off a paper I'd been writing,
entitled *Hallucinogenic drugs and their effect on literary imagination.*

Extract from The Mermaid, traditional version by Andrew Draskoy.

It'll all come out in the wash

I wash my hair in washing-up liquid,
it saves the pennies while making it curl.
I thought it would make me look the part,
as a roadie with a band called Everything But The Girl.

I'd joined after I was kicked out from my teaching post
at Mulchester Marton public school,
after broadcasting radical views over the school radio.

I was vilified by the PC brigade and called an 'old fart',
after mentioning Billy Bunter,
every kid's favourite fictional doughnut-crunching hero.

I loved those stories and had a schoolmate just like Billy did,
an Indian lad, whom I'd nicknamed 'Hurree Ramjet Singh',
after Billy's brown-skinned classmate.

We played music together and our single *I'm Fat And He's Nearly Black*,
was a hit on Radio Caroline.

Apparently it was inspired by Hurree being lambasted by the insult beginning with P.

'Dammit,' he said, 'I'm not even from Pakistan.'

So, he went off to Ireland and played with harpist Sorcha McFee,
who'd caused controversy by declaring her love for a Gypsy woman.

I mentioned this tale when I was interviewed by the magazine, *Melody Maker*,
laughing at how my musical career ended when I realised I couldn't sing.

The young journalist gave me a funny look, because tales of Billy Bunter
and Irish folkies were not what she considered 'cool',
even if they did contain an ethnic lad called Hurree Ramjet Singh.

I was by then seen as the 'man in the know' when talking about 1980s bands,
having written a biopic about my time with a band that rhymes with swirl.

So, the interviewer was flummoxed when I expressed annoyance
at her attitude.

The resulting furore, which went all over a new
phenomenon called social media, set me on a path to celebrity status,
after I'd been asked to advertise Vosene, based on my nomenclature.

Is that the right word? Look at the bottom of the page, to check my moniker.

However, I discovered to my shock it's a real product and am now negotiating
to avoid legal action from a maker of shampoo.

Alternatively, I will team up with my old pal Hurree,
who's returned from Erin's isle,
having made a fortune with Miss Breen and their song,
W*e Don't fit In, Aren't We Cool?*

So, sorry to cut this short, but I'm due in court after a maker of hair products
has threatened to sue..

Their sales have dropped alarmingly, people preferring to use
what makes their dishes sparkle.

I will plead, 'This all started when I used washing-up
liquid to make my hair curl'.

Bum look doesn't make a woman for our times

She doesn't have a Beyoncé bum, that Miss Too-Good-By-Moonlight,'
my sister observed, referring to a woman with an odd pseudonym,
after accusing me of ogling a photograph-laden blog on the world-wide-web,
whose strands were spreading across my chest, saying,
'What a flighty madame, pontificating on subjects
she's no right to discuss.'

I woke up with a start, then quickly asked for a drink
from the steward on the Johannesburg to London flight.

The realisation I had suffered that old nightmare again – sparked by the
recurring memory of those villains I'd encountered
on the high veldt, particularly one,
laughing wickedly under a leopard-skin hat,
while I cowered under a prickly bush – hit me like a cold shower.

I realised I needed to go Ireland again,
to that island off the coast of county Clare, and relax in that eccentric hostel,
A Refuge Of Quiet Retreat, bedecked with gaudy paintings of
men who just looked at me.

It was run by a transgenderist called Brian, and his sister, Beatitude,
a former marketing executive who still spoke like it,
despite claiming to have embraced an earthier existence,
whom the locals would gossip about as 'that little lesbo'.

I was welcomed by that 'very cool' pair who I'm ashamed to admit,
irritated me with their cliche-driven phrases,
her constantly 'going forward', like a government minister at a press
conference and her football-mad 'bruv',
forever getting 'a result', looking backwards at days of sporting glory.

I laughed when I was gently chided for calling her 'luv',
saying, 'I'm from Lancashire,

and that's an example of dialect', but her brother reluctantly agreed with me,
as he was from the Yorkshire town of Middlefeckan,
and could not quite forget inter-county rivalry.

That night I had that dream again – wearing a vest and shorts,
in which I was chased by a lion,
competing in a championship cross-country race,
while the two hostel owners were watching,
Brian shouting, 'Nice legs', and I responded,
'Yes, but shame about the face.'

To which he answered, 'No darling, you're gorgeous.'

Then to my relief I saw my father elbow him away, whispering,
'He's straight, I sent him to conversion therapy.'

Then he shouted, 'Come on son, you're flying!'

I smiled through the pain when I heard him, knowing that as a kid
he'd really wanted me to bend a ball, like that fellow Beckham.

But he knew I couldn't control one,
and athletics was good for my mental health,
even though I did occasionally score an own goal

The next day I was strolling along the strand,
when I heard a snatch of that enchanting song,
The First Time Ever I Saw Your Face.

Then I saw Miss Too-Good-By-Moonlight on a rocky prominence,
wearing that leopard-skin pelted hat,
being ogled by my argumentative friend from the place I'd retreated to,
so I ran away to the cliff edge.

Was she following me, I wondered,
along with her rival Magical Multi-layered Madge,
another daft pseudonym, who boasted an even
better blog wherein she dices with death,
herding ostriches on the South African Karoo?

Then they both took me for a naked dip where we just swam,
and I told them about my dream.

Miss What's-her-name, with the nomenclature
ending in Moonlight – suggested I take up mindfulness,
a form of meditation used to clear the mind,
while Madge said 'I use that technique,
it's good, and can I lie next to you?'

I considered this request and, after a quiet chat,
she shook hands with her rival,
and all three of us meditated enough to conjure an image of us
drifting away on imaginary beds of feathers,
carolled by harmonious sea gulls,
their beaks filled with baby seals who did a comedy routine,
full of non-PC gags, with Mick,
Pat and a Glaswegian called Jimmy,
while we sipped wine and played charades
(I was James Bond, finally lying with Miss Moneypenny).

Waking up, I said to the steward, 'Can I have the same again?'

By the way, he did have a Beyoncé bum.

Padraig and the Bushwacker

She was known as the Bushwhacker, scourge of elephant
hunters of the Transvaal, since her beloved Dolly Big Ears
was taken for her tusks.

However, she fell in love with one such killer, Padraig O'Reilly,
a sergeant of The Irish Guards, who vowed to himself,
'She's a right pretty gal, I want to marry her; yes, I truly must.

'I hope she'll forgive me for slaughtering her beloved creatures elephantine,
a trade I only took up to feed myself after deserting my regiment.'

The bushwhacker soon learned that her lover had become
a fugitive since he struck his colonel, Simpson Sup-Lightly,
after he'd damned the men of Dublin's Easter rebellion.

For Padraig was torn between the oath of loyalty to an English
monarch and the dream his old mother often sang, of a united Ireland.

So he had pledged support for the rebels,
then deserted before he could be executed at dawn.

But the little bushwhacker felt her heart leap when she heard him whistling,
I'll Take You Home Again Kathleen, and she laughed as he talked about his
childhood in the village of Rathcoomb.

But the romantic spell was broken by a rifle shot,
as another animal was killed for sport,
and the two rode for the safety of the Drakensberg Mountains.

There they met Simpson Sup-Lightly, the former colonel,
bathing under one of the place's many waterfalls.

His batman, Michael Monkeaton, told them,
'The colonel's going to turn these into water fountains,
and transform this delightful dell into a sanctuary for old soldiers.'

Padraig was startled to hear a shout 'Hello sergeant!',
and saw his formerly immaculately-attired officer sporting a beard
and long hair, who declared, 'Welcome, I've had a revelation,
that you young Padraig are a missionary, but don't know it.

'I dreamt that all my former transgressions would be forgiven,
if I shook the hand of a soldier I had once disciplined,
because I suffer from guilt and want to clear my conscience.'

The bushwhacker and the sergeant listened,
as the colonel declared his desire for a world where there no wars,
and volunteered for a mission to spread love around
the magnificent country of South Africa,
a state bedevilled by violence.

They disappeared for many years, but last week a
travelling salesman in bullet-proof vests
told the British consulate he'd seen a couple answering their
description being pursued by a posse of politicians,
who were crying 'Peace and love is all very well for the tourists,
but it's not good for our careers.

Dashitall, we should have listened to him!

People don't listen to me any more, now that after the
army coup our country has a new regime.

Indeed, they call me an old bore who sits in a bar,
while everyone's watching football,
lamenting 'It all changed when we lost the old Queen.'

I would tell the young 'uns about the bravest man I ever knew,
Endacott Dashitall, whom I met talking to a tree on top of Mulligawtanny Hill.

He was a wizard with children, his long beard emphasising
his fantastical stories; ah, I can see him still.

The dads thought him weird but, unusual in a village so conservative,
he was a hit with the mums, but rumours abound of his past,
how he was a witness to horrible scenes.

It seemed he'd fought for 'king and country', and on return was expected to
follow his father and run the family estate, but shocked everyone by
saying he'd embraced Karl Marx, condemning his government's sharp
swing to the political right.

A keen musician, he formed a folk band called The Strumming Chums,
and I remember him telling me that was how he'd met his fiancée,
as he sang Woody Guthrie protest songs outside the
USAAF air base at Upper Manningford,
where they were beaten up by representatives of our government's
lurch into what they call 'a new ordered world'.

It was there he met Flight Lieutenant Mary Lou, who admired his playing,
confessing she used to strum and play, back home in Tennessee,
saying, 'I'm a great fan of Woody.'

'Indeed,' he concurred, 'the voice of the dispossessed people.

'And here you are, coming out of a place that has enough explosives
to make those huge dust-bowl winds he sang about look mighty feeble.'

'Oh, you're a radical then?'

She countered, 'But this is a violent world,
and we need to defend our nation.'

'But you're on the soil of England, and I prefer to ward
off enemies with music and song.'

She laughed, 'You should manage that easily, the way you sing!'

A year later Mary Lou and Endicott were gazing into each other's eyes,
their police handcuffs preventing too much physical
ardour in their cold cell.

When they tried a kiss, guards rushed in and indulged in
what looked like a rugby maul.

'You're a right chump,' she declared,
and Enders laughed at her somewhat less than angry expression,
as she continued, 'I represented the USAAF at baseball,
so you should have let me throw that egg at President Trump.'

At which Endacott rebuked her 'I told you that man was a fraud.'

'Yes, but it would have spoiled his suit, apparently it cost two grand.'

'Indeed,' he laughed, 'Right, let's sing Woody Guthrie's
anthem for the people, *This Land Is Our Land.*

Which was the last thing my old pal heard
before they faced the firing squad.

The downfall of private Muldoon

I've met many characters at Alcoholics Anonymous,
their spark fading due to the necessity for sobriety,
but none were as ridiculously talented as Michael Muldoon.

His arrival at our meeting came because of his success as a sports star and movie stuntman.

So why then, I wondered, did he end up in a hotel
with a revolver next to a bottle of whisky?

Which is the heart-rending story he told us, his honesty cutting us to the quick.

When I pressed him, his explanation did not convince me – was he
being entirely truthful, blaming noted philanthropist
Major-General Bertram Bunty-Bronson for his downfall?

But I am getting ahead of myself – I shall step back in time to when a
young Private Muldoon first met the aforementioned Bronson,
then a distinguished British Army officer on liaison
with the Irish Army in county Donegal,
his contact with said force being a Major Wills Wilde-Finnegan,
who resented the Britisher's presence, especially after he'd claimed he could revolutionise his battalion.

Wills thus laughed when Bunty-Bronson made himself look a fool,
when he led a route march to Dunnybannion,
and was kicked on the bottom by a mule.

But Bertie, as Bunty-Bronson was affectionately known,
seemed a kindly aristocratic buffer.

However, Muldoon's mum warned him, 'I have the gift of foresight,
and he has mind-bending ways.'

But her son was swept along by the general warmth
expressed towards the officer.

'He's not all like some English fellows,' the Irish soldiers all agreed.

'Indeed,' they cried, 'What about the fella from Geordie land,
who coached our football team to a win over the auld enemy?'

'Actually,' Bunty pointed out, 'it was Sunderland, so he wasn't a Geordie.'

But private Muldoon declared, 'But Jack's the patron saint of Ireland,
God be praised!'

The major looked shocked, 'What do you mean, private?
That's blasphemous.'

At which the soldier laughed, 'I jest Sir.

'I was making a comparison to what John Lennon said, tongue in cheek,
about the Beatles being more important than Jesus.'

'Ah I see.

'You mean this land of saints and scholars
has less interest in its famous saint, and more in a game of football?

'Well, I'm a rugby man myself.'

The private looked intrigued, 'League or union?'

'Union, but I am an admirer of Jason Robinson, and watched him
when he was a Pie Eater.'

The private laughed, 'You mean Wigan?'

'That's correct, Muldoon.'

The private fancied himself as a rugby speedster and Bronson was soon putting
him through his paces, running over ploughed fields
with a sack of potatoes, racing his dog,
appropriately nicknamed Dashing Darcy,
after his favourite fictional historical character,
Darcy-Dregs from a novel by Jane Austin.

The dog's athletic ability gave the troop a merry weekend in the capital,
when they bet on it competing in the fiercely competitive Oscar Wilde Stakes,
confounding the bookies when she turned up, tripping over her long legs,
seemingly very much, to quote an appropriate metaphor 'Not at the races!'

It transpired that this was an effect induced by Muldoon's uncle,
Pat 'The Mind Bender' Hypnotistic Muldoon,
who was hiding from Inspector 'Clueful' McCabe,
fresh from nabbing a drug gang.

Praised by the Taoiseach and lauded in the press,
Muldoon treated himself to a night's gambling,
but suspected something was amiss, when the lifeless
dog dashed off at speed, and great joy was expressed by the
soldiers knocking back beer in the cheap stand.

From then on the money rolled in, as he and Pat cornered the market in
greyhound nobbling, then a thriving underworld practice.

It was through this that he met one Dougie Wetherall,
who incidentally had served under a certain major-general
who bought him out of the army,
and the ex-footslogger was soon being coached to
be a winger for Bradford Northern rugby league team.

They dominated the competition, even putting the
rugby union hierarchy's nose out of joint,
by winning the Twickenham Sevens.

Watching in the VIP area was his former superior,
Major-General Bertram Bunty-Bronson,
and was seen after the game exchanging money
with a disreputable character,
who looked very like Muldoon's uncle,
Pat 'The Mind Bender' Hypnotistic Muldoon,
lately of the state prison at Monasterevin,
but now avoiding the law by calling himself Jeremiah Jempson,
a born-again Christian preacher selling paperback *Bibles*.

Coincidentally he'd met his nephew prior to the game,
which he scored 10 tries in, scouring through the opposition.

Then in *The Times* it was announced that a noted British Army
officer had acquired the Hampdown estate,
complete with racing stables.

One night, many years later, Muldoon was relaxing
in the bar of the Winsome Winger, where he was hailed as a hero,
with pictures of his try-scoring feats,
plus images from the films he'd been a stuntman in,
including *Nightfall*, a B-movie sequel to the Bond one *Skyfall*,
when in walked his old mentor, Major-General Bertram Bunty-Bronson.

After several hours of reminiscing, the ex-officer came to the point,
'Remember that Irish Army officer, Major Wills Wilde-Finnegan?

'Well, to put his nose out I courted his daughter, and employed
her as a barmaid at my stately-home's bar, serving our ale,
amusingly called Swithin's Swill.

'Well, her dad found out and blackmailed me,
so to come up with the necessary funds I teamed
up with your uncle Pat – however,
I've just found out that he hypnotised me.'

At this Muldoon said 'Well, he is a hypnotist.'

Indeed, 'What a character that fellow is, he's a true genius,
and he taught me how to make people do things against their will.'

The rest is history, which is why that former rugby star and stuntman
ended up in a group where everyone prefers to remain anonymous.

Nursing a broken heart

'Well,' I mused to myself in my despair, 'that's it,
she's found herself a man, he's more mature and bigger of frame
than what I am, and now I'm left alone.'

Indulgent self-pitying maybe.
So I reflected on my love life, I'd had admirers but no partakers
in the court of romance, just like a newly-crowned king on his throne.

One particular, dressed so alluring in a nurse's uniform,
used to glance towards me at the bus stop, but never punched my ticket,
and I was dismayed when I saw her with a well-built man
who bought this lady a pint in a sports bar,
but all he seemed to do was watch the cricket.

Many men have cast similar glances at my object of desire,
even a Hong Kong contortionist called the Snap Dragon,
but their affair ended when he told her, 'I'm all tied up, I can't make it.'

How life turns, I mused in my hospital bed, bruised and battered after
some ageing rocker had told me off for drinking coffee instead of beer,
after a session in the Blues Bar
Maybe I was still suffering from concussion, but I'm sure I saw my bus-stop
acquaintance knock my assailant out with a neat one-two.

For I'd woken up in a hospital bed, rather light headed,
to see the object of my desire, acting in her nursing capacity.

She asked 'Have you been?'
I answered, bemused, 'Yes, but not a number two.'

'Oh, I'll give you some dates.'

Before she went, I asked, 'How's your boyfriend with the muscles?'

She looked surprised, then replied,
'Oh him, that's my personal trainer, but he's as camp as a field of tents'.
The next day I saw her at the bus stop, and we had lots of the above.

Les – the 'fool' with the tool

They called him Lusty Les, the chap who ran
round the 'bare-it-all' beaches of Cornwall,
naked but for an Arabian fez wielding a spanner,
his favourite tool.

He wanted the female bathers to see his muscled body,
but they were all in the bar of the
Old Cornwallians Women's Rugby Club,
which had kindly let them use the showers,
due to a plumbing emergency at the naturists' camp,
even though the president, Mrs Dashwood-Dalrymple,
was a confessed prude.

They laughed when he appeared with his spanner,
which he'd announced on the club's Facebook page
was his favourite implement,
and could fix any blockage, leak or plumbing appendage.

When Les duly fixed the leaking faucet,
he became an honorary member of this emerging women's club,
who loved to play rugby union football.

The women, led by feisty forward Babs Bushdimple,
exclaimed 'Les, you're a fool!'

'Oh' he answered, 'I like to reveal most of everything where it is appropriate,
like on this lovely beach,
but I like dressing up to watch you ladies play rugby football.'

Years later, the fairer sex are now playing both rugby codes,
but when Old Cornwallians Women's Rugby Club
qualified to compete in the English Ladies Championship,
a last-minute drama threatened when the showers broke down,
and both teams refused to take the pitch.

When Les, a keen travelling fan, offered
his services Major-General (retired)
Gerald Gillinsgate dismissed him as a 'fool',
calling in his own man who'd served with him in The Welsh Guards,

known among his old pals as 'Taff The Tap Taffy',
but try as he might couldn't resolve the problem,
losing his temper and calling Les an 'idiot'.

But with the big game imminent, common sense prevailed and Lesley
wielded his favourite tool to tweak the 'what-you-m'call' it.

His memory is celebrated at that Cornish Women's Rugby Club as the man,
known as 'The fool with the tool', now married to Babs,
who no longer regards him as a freak,
after he and his trusty spanner ensured that she and her teammates,
when they took the field at Twickenham – and,
this comment is made tongue in cheek – would have
what all women must have – a shower.

Little Rob, the greatest littlest scrum half

As a young 'un Little Rob was told he was too small,
considering he was five-foot nothing,
to run and score with the oval ball.

But he wouldn't listen and forged his own path in the 13-aside game,
much maligned in this country,
where soccer reigns supreme.

He brought a smile to the hearts of us rugby leaguers,
as he made the opposition big lads wish
they could take an 'early bath'.

I saw him in the bar after the match, and thought he was a school boy,
instead of the greatest, littlest scrum half.

When the pressure was on in the Superleague Grand Final,
he scuttled under the grasp of a big forward,
to score the one that got his team the trophy,
that day at the iconic Old Trafford.

But now he is fighting the cruel hand of fate,
with the same energetic fury as when he took the field,
refusing to accept he's beat,
with the help of the rugby league faithful,
and the legend that is Sir Kevin Sinfield.

Rocky road to Jesus

She was a ruddy-faced nun, banished to a convent to cure her
habit of singing cheeky songs, where she met Sister Superior McPeake,
who saw in her a talent for musical theatre,
so turned a blind eye so the novice could sneak
out at night to star in *The Rocky Horror Show.*

But one night, sobbing in the street, because she'd realised that Christ
was her only true love, she gazed at the stars and said,
'Please protect my sisters, who have gone to the war-torn Congo.

'I will join them soon, after I take my final bow.
But I will have to tell my suitor, *Strictly Come Dancing* star Sam Shufflesong,
that I can't be his bride, and I know he'll be furious.'

But not long after, lying in a hospital in a Congolese jungle near death,
she was alarmed to hear theatrical voices sing
'We'll have nun of that lying in bed,
get up and sing, you know it's good for your health,
and besides, we need a lead in our chorus.'

The next day the holy woman was entertaining village children,
who just loved her choice of rock n' roll, that she'd learned
on that rocking horror musical extravaganza,
*The Rocky Horror Sho*w, when a man jumped out of a thicket,
crying 'Follow me!' and they escaped the rebel forces,
soon reaching a deep river.

There were a few who couldn't swim, saying 'Help me Lord,'
but were suddenly felt imbued with aquatic ability.

Reaching safety, they waved at the soldiers they'd escaped from who,
when they saw a figure rise out of the water holding a cross,
put down their guns and refused to follow their captain,
pleading – at the risk of a firing squad – 'Sir, we are reared to
follow the Christian God,
and this miraculous event has made us mighty curious.'

Then everyone stared in awe, when the singing nun shouted,
'It's that much maligned uncool fellow called Jesus.'

He's football crazy

'Is the round-ball game the opium of the people?'
I asked that humanitarian chap, Gary Linebreaker.

'I don't know,' he looked dumbfounded, 'I'll have to put that
question to my expert summariser, Billy 'Fire it in' Beagle.'

All he could say was, 'We should play a 3 4 2 3 formation, going forward.'

But Gary interjected, 'But a 2 3 4 5 1 one would see us going backward.'

Sounds daft? Well it was a dream, prompted by
listening to BBC Radio 5 Live,
whose presenters seemed to punctuate every discussion
with references to football,
before getting to grips with the topic of the day,
climate change – the biggest danger facing mankind,
not to mention the beloved bee, who due to unseasonal temperatures
is staying longer in its beehive.

Then top presenter Mark Hanmacker,
whose favourite music is hip hop (I know, 'cos he mentions it
every time he's on), oh, and that he's a football fan
(as does his colleague, Fabian Piles
who tells his audience he follows West Bromwich Albion)
introduced the show with another lament about the
fortunes of his favourite club,
while looking enviously at that other team - you know the one,
with its stand called the Kop - whose average expenditure
would triple that of third-world countries like
Myanmar and Africa's Lesotho.

So I wondered, is something sinister going on at
BBC Broadcasting House?

Are they all getting VIP tickets to Tottenham, Arsenal and Chelsea,
and that new team funded by two Hollywood stars, Wimbley Water FC,
an amalgamation of Wimbledon and Waterloo?

'They need better players, I know a few,'
claimed experienced manager Jimmy Takeanap,
and there was a pause as he looked for gum to chew,
which he manufactured at his appropriately-named
Chew-it-all company in Fulham.

'After all,' he muttered, 'I have to keep up my image.'

Then I heard scratching at the door, and in walked Mickey Mouse.

I asked him, 'Do you want some past-its-sell-by-date spinach?'

He grinned, 'Yes please.
I lived on these before I got my break in film.'

'I left Walt Disney, not because I was called a 'rodent' by a chief executive,
upset 'cos I'd eaten all the cheese, but over them constantly
talking about football, which bored me silly.

'So, when they accused me of taking the Mickey, I felt I had to go.'

I again cocked an ear to Five Live, and heard Mark Hanmacker
ask 'What next for Spurs?'

'Well,' answered Wally Theostot, 'first of all,
they have to start winning football matches,'
which received a witty rejoinder from left-wing academic,
Irishman John Jodhpurs, waiting in the green room before being
interviewed about famous author George Orwell,
who invented the phrase 'Big Brother is watching you'.

John commented on Wally's verdict, 'I thought that was the idea.
Does he think they should win rugby games?'

But hidden microphones picked up this acerbic dig,
and to make matters worse,
his interview got off to a bad start when he was asked,
'What football team do you follow?'

His answer was surprising, 'Mighty Munster.'

There followed a strained silence, 'Never heard of 'em!'

'They're a top GAA team,' replied the writer.

'But that's not football,' answered a flustered Mark,
wishing he was on a commercial station and could save
his blushes by going to an ad break.

'It is, but not as you know it,' shouted the next guest,
sitting in the green room, waiting to come on and talk
about a book he'd written about US sci-fi TV series *Star Trek*.

This was really getting to the radio host, so he put on a hip-hop tune
(forgetting he was on 'serious' radio, and not in a night club in Ibiza)
in an effort to restore calm.

As for the George Orwell expert, he felt this was all becoming too Orwellian,
and, feeling it was time to beat a retreat, addressed the radio show host
(who was thinking, 'I hope this doesn't go to extra time')
asking him 'Is the Beeb Big Brother, and really is watching you?'
then escaped to his Co. Kildare home,
with his cattle and sheep, appropriately called *Animal Farm*.

A novel experience

My story begins the night Heathcliff, that handsome
literary invention of one half of the Bronte sisters,
popped his head into my tent above Withens Moor,
saying, 'Budge over, she's kicked me out.

'I've been carousing at The Sleepy Shepherd,' I announced,
'with my literary creator Emily, but her sister Charlotte turned up,
and she doesn't half like her pints of stout.'

Filled with fear at this apparition, I hastily decamped to Oxenhope
with its historic trains, from where I steamed along the Worth Valley,
imagining those cinematic *Railway Children* leaping from the pages
of Edith Nesbitt's novel, at the quaint Oakworth station.

Feeling nostalgic I headed for Stoodley Pike,
with its monument standing like a sentinel,
which I – in that glorious summer long ago during when I'd
smashed personal bests at athletic meets – had once raced over,
using my speed over the weather-beaten Pennine rocks,

I recalled how my father – a hospital chiropodist,
taking a break from disinfected wards and corny feet – cheered
me on as I competed in Todmorden Harriers' fell race on a balmy summer night.

But now in my senior years I can only think about the past,
along with my unheralded guest,
who's now back at my tent, stinking of ale and unwashed socks.

He's a true restless spirit, floating around waiting for love
letters and forget-me-nots.

Then, after 'Heathy' woke up screaming for the umpteenth time,
I asked, 'Can't you see a therapist?'

'Therapy has limited success,' he replied, 'you told me so yourself.'

That night I visited the Sleepy Shepherd to meet Heathy,
who was due to fly over on an angelic flight.

As I walked in, Kate Bush's hit song filled the pub with its haunting air,
and we sang along to her beautiful ballad, *Wuthering Heights.*

'I've always loved that song,' I said to the bar man,
who looked at me, saying, 'Don't I know you?'

Weren't you a psychiatrist at our mental hospital, Stoodley View?
There was a rumour you left under a cloud.'

But Heathy saved my embarrassment, as he declared,

'Oh, there you are! I wanted to say thanks for encouraging
me to sort myself out.

'Oh, and for washing my socks.

'I've made it up with the ghostly Brontes, and am attending a
writing class called Paradise Write Aloud.'

'There's a load of literary geniuses helping – Conan Doyle
of Sherlock Holmes fame, and Joseph Conrad, you know,
Heart of Darkness, The N Word Of The Narcissus?

'They're a sort of charitable collective,
helping spirits with a literary bent.

'I'm going to become a ghostwriter,
and I'll be haunting your dreams again, if not your tent.'

Seeking to escape I sought the jukebox and Kate Bush's lovely lyrics.
After treating myself to a whisky, the bar man said,
'I remember, you were a big drinker and kept some funny company.'

I replied, 'Well, I've always been partial to spirits.'

Billy Bob And The Vibrating Skeleton

I am a hail-fellow-well-met Victorian gent of some renown,
who lost his top hat but was cheered when it was located at the lost and found.

The topper was handed in by Marvellous Madge,
a contortionist with Freddy Follodop's Travelling Circus,
led by the impresario Michael O'Flaherty,
who thought up such a mouthful after being
administered a heavy dose of bicarbonate of soda
to combat an embarrassing attack of flatus.

This O'Flaherty boasted of Madge's undying love,
every night in the snug at the Admiral Lord Nelson.

But unknown to him the said supple lady was entranced by another,
from that very same travelling troupe, called Billy Bob,
The Vibrating Skeleton.

Being a man of influence, I booked the secret lovers to
appear at the British Bulldogs dinner.

Alas, if only I'd known the heartache my generous act would cause.

They wowed the genteel audience with a joint show of shuddering bones,
invoking rapturous applause.

Just as I was about to offer a heartfelt congratulation,
the doors flew open to admit a brass band from the Methodist Chapel,
intent on acquiring a flock of new souls.

Madge was filled with awe at their brass neck and
shining belief in the Almighty,
which to her seemed to be saying: 'Come with us and
follow the path to salvation,
and escape from your servitude under that devious sod O'Flaherty.'

Throughout this concert of holy angels, a distinguished cove with a Tennessee
accent and wideawake hat had been boasting of his vast fortune,
in between regaling everyone with tales of Wild West adventure.

She soon discovered this boastful gent
was an agent for Perky Pontague's Peculiar Performers,
and allowed herself to be plied with
pints of Bassets Beautiful Ale, awaking to find she was
booked in a touring show called Weird and Wacky Wonders.

This extraordinary production boasted pantomime elephants,
dancing dervishes and a singing swan.

Billy Bob was heartbroken at losing his sweetheart, and set off in pursuit,
busking his unique act, occasionally being paid in kind,
notably in the fair city of Dublin,
where he found refuge in Ma Murphy's House Of Ill Repute.

Here he learned that Madge, after stealing a leading lady's Portmanteau,
had been kicked out of Pontague's wacky troupe,
where she'd performed with a clown called Laughing Pat MacBunnion,
whose bestselling act was to produce cards out of his huge behind,
all done with the aid of a midget hiding in his voluminous three-piece suit.

At first laughing Pat was hostile to Billy's enquiries,
until he remembered the note given to him by Gervase O'Rafferty,
whom he had begged to help him locate his lost love.

'Have a pint of stout,' he exclaimed,
'and I'll tell you how that rascal Gervase and I smuggled poteen
under the noses of the Royal Irish Constabulary,
then you can persuade your lady friend to stop trying to sell
me barrels of Basset's Beautiful Ale.

'She's a lovely lady, but on that subject is fast becoming a bore.

'I tried said beverage when I played in O'Bunnion's Bouncing Banjos,
on a rare trip to Albion's shore, and it really is, to use a phrase
which originated in this fair city, 'beyond the pale'.

'If I was you I'd forget her, for she longs for a life you can't provide,
but rather desires Lord Gervase Golighty to promenade by her side,
and later', he said with a wink, 'demonstrating her
contortionist skills beneath his freshly-scented sheets'.

But Billy clung to his romantic illusions, until one night,
leaving O'Monaghan's Music Hall, where he had deputised for Gob's Gillican,
the Shimmering Shadow, he met the full force of one Rufus Roughshod,
a 20-stone bruiser from Woolwich Arsenal,
ex-sergeant to former Colonel Golightly, who left him with the warning
'Forget that woman, nor your bones will vibrate no more.'

'What's it to you?' Cried Billy Bob,
'You're of humble stock, and your master's part of the ruling class.'

'You're right lad,' he replied.

'But I owe him, for he saved me from certain death in the Indian Mutiny,
when we sacked a temple at Madras, and I nearly paid the ultimate price,
for trying to pinch a prince's jewel-encrusted chamber pot.'

Billy's cries alerted a passing gypsy caravan,
whose ancient mother pumped him full of herbal infusions.

Then, taken by the Romany tribe on their road south,
he set up his own magical show,
in a cave deep in the Kerry mountains known
as The MacGillycuddy Reeks.

His remarkable talents left the children in hysterics,
but rumours emerged about a ghostly woman,
whose heart-rending sobs were often heard as Billy counted his daily fortune.

A scientist from the British institute for Atmospherical Spooks
and Spirits - ASS for short,
said it was the cave's geophysical atmospherics,
which permeated Billy Bob's Magical Emporium.

But rumours persisted that it was one Margaret Williams,
stage name Marvellous Madge,
who in an effort to escape her bankrupt husband,
was lost overboard on the Dublin packet boat
still keening for her lost love, Billy Bob,
The Vibrating Skeleton.

The Vicar Of Beacon's Bottom

The Reverend Miss P, who for years had cheerfully warded the
attentions from the men of her parish,
invited me on one of her well-organised rambles.

Later I watched as she tucked into her lasagne in The Peckish Partridge,
a pub she insisted we go to, rather than that other hostelry, The Feisty Farmer.

It has, as she pointed out, 'Pictures of busty
women admiring a sweaty blacksmith,' and then declared,
'Images like that endorse the myth of the domineering male.'

To disguise my surprise at this outburst, I teased her about the calories
contained in said meal.

But she retorted with a diatribe about her achievements
as a Beacon's Bottom Harrier, then made me feel like a couch
potato when she listed her weekly running mileage.

I was further impressed when she said, 'So I think you'll agree that I'm entitled
to a good feed...' but our conversation was interrupted by Miles Manningport,
a wealthy landowner, who, with his comments,
indicated there was history between the two of them.

When I tactfully asked if they had been an item, she simply said, 'He was so
boring.

'All he did was talk about sheep dips and silage.'

Then changed the subject by advising me to
read her pamphlet on that holy figure, the Venerable Bede.

This cute cleric was a breath of fresh air, compared to the others
I'd met in my shady career with her Majesty's Government – all city types,
particularly my ex-wife, a typical pretend socialist,
who laughed when I hinted I was some sort of secret agent,
saying, 'You're just a plain old data analyst.'

So I again joined the vicar's rambling group to climb Montague's Mount,
that impressive monument to our glorious dead which
overlooked my new home of Beacon's Bottom.

As we strode along, I was ready to impress her with quotes
from her book on The Bede, when she suddenly sat down and swore,
with c and f words flowing with equal abandonment.

I was intrigued by this, as I'd heard that eccentricity
was not unknown among her antecedents.

It seemed that her great aunt, Mrs Bunty Babstock-Bunsen,
had performed heroic deeds in the Indian Mutiny,
inspiring the English defenders in the besieged Cawnpore cantonment,
and written a best-selling book,
A Rebellious Woman Of A Conformist Century,
which tells how her eccentric aunt had
brought an Indian mystic with her to England,
who would sit on the highest branch of an ancient beech,
in this very village, and perform the Indian rope trick,
then sell his Life Affirming Soup, which, I quote,
'Is made from the leaves of our ancient tree.

'So take a sip and amaze everyone with your mystically-induced self confidence.'

But the leader of the parish council, Godfrey Love-broad,
claimed all it did was give him flatulence.

In an article in the *Beacon's Bugle* he warned,
'This foreign interloper is perpetrating a fraud.'

However, a notoriously shy solicitor, Lionel Lovelorn,
suddenly came out of his shell after a diet of Old Knobbly soup,
and took up the cause of the much maligned Hindu,
successfully suing Godfrey and announced,

'For years I have been stricken by the curse of shyness.

'But now, to use a metaphor, I no longer sit in the wings,
but strut on the stage of life, doing what the other chaps do.

'Indeed, as the psychologists say, I am happy within myself,
and outside of it well – I'm a bleeding extrovert!'

But the council leader muttered, 'He sounds pissed.'

Then shouted, 'You're more like a bloody pervert!'

'Now then Godfrey...' Lionel laughed,
then spoiled his outburst with an untimely belch.

'Anyway,' he continued, 'I have joined our
village's amateur dramatics group,
and we'll be staging that saucy romp,
A Funny Thing Happened On The Way To The Forum.'

There was a murmur of disapproval.

'Yes, isn't that right, Mrs Montrose Montgomery-Marston?'
He asked, looking pointedly at the stage director of the Players,
who nodded agreeably, but muttered under breath,
'Dashed upstart doesn't have any talent.

'He's taking the lead part for himself.'

'Anyway,' commented her husband, 'the vicar would object.

'She's such a straight-laced madam.'

However, a decided kink was observed in Miss P's hitherto laces,
after she saw a comic sketch entitled *The Sex Lives Of The Plantagenets,*
which highlighted the story of a 15th-century lady-in-waiting,
who donned a joker's outfit, thus becoming the very first alternative comedian.

As she preferred women in tights to men in clinking armour,
this amazing woman became known on the underground comedy circuit,
secretly supported by HRH Elizabeth, The Virgin Queen,
as Pamela Pouncy – The Perverted Poltroon.

Who, according to Miss P's genealogy expert,
was a predecessor to her great aunt, Mrs Bunty Babstock-Bunsen.

I learned all this during our walk, as Miss P
indulged in a burst of loquaciousness,
while sipping from a cup of an odd-smelling soup.

And then she dropped her bombshell, that she'd relented in her opposition
to staging that saucy play, *A Funny Thing Happened
On The Way To The Forum*, and had even joined the cast.

But there was a snag, as she explained,
'I couldn't resist giving the younger
actors' strict moral codes to follow in their quest for romance.

'However, I must have put that old know-all,
Mrs Montgomery-Marston's nose out of joint.
I can imagine the conversation she had with her husband.

"*I've had three sons, what does that stuck-up vicar know about life*?"

Old Monty would probably reply thus:

*'Indeed. Gervase is a merchant banker who never visits;
Chrispin's an actor baring his arse in some hippy musical,
who does visit, but was caught by PC Milliken smoking pot!*

*'Then there's Monkton, a celebrity therapist, who thinks everything's cool,
whom some gossip columnist christened Philpot The Piss Pot,
'cos he's like that silly sod Manningport – a right old lush.*
…………………………………………………………………………

The sun was setting as we finished our walk,
but Marjorie Mumps and Major (retired), Fred Thistle-Pile,
took such an agonising time to conclude their farewells,
that I tried to slink off, so I wouldn't be invited to join them at the Ring O'Bells.

However, Miss P caught me as I slunk behind a bush, saying,
'Oh you're having a pee.

‘Don’t worry, they’ve gone.

‘We can admire the sunset from Old Knobbly; oh, do come!’

‘Did you know this is where my great aunt’s Indian
mystic created his self-liberating soup?’

She asked, jumping onto a lower branch, saying,

‘There’s plenty of space up here, come on, jump up!’

‘Oh yes,’ I answered, ‘I’ve never had any of his famous concoction.’

Then she announced, looking at me strangely, ‘I had some for lunch.
Don’t worry about Miles.

‘I know things about him that he’s managed to keep secret.’

‘Really?’

‘My cousin was in the athletics team at Oxford with him,
and he would wear his mum’s underwear in competitions.’

She giggled. ‘He claimed they were easier on his nether regions.’

She suddenly fixed a gaze on me.
‘So, what are your thoughts on mystics, fairies, shape shifters,
those hidden forces that live in that hinterland
between reality and the subconscious?’

I thought for a second, ‘Well, one should never dismiss the possibility
that there is a force up there seeking to create a more spiritual man.’

I was quite impressed by my off-the-cuff answer, then she answered,
‘Yes, but I’m a woman.’

A week later I was still nursing the bruise I sustained that day when we
fell off the tree still engaged in a passionate kiss,
but was as happy as the proverbial Larry,

at the news that had quickly gone around the village,
that its odd vicar was to be known as my missus.

Meanwhile, when the news of our coming nuptials was announced,
Mrs Montgomery-Marston was heard to mutter,
'Now I know she's lost the plot!'

At the opening night of the play I was adjusting my toga,
when in came a drunken Miles.

'How are you feeling?' He asked.

'Nervous,' I answered.

He laughed, 'You shouldn't be, haven't you already been
where no man has gone before?'

A second later I was remembering the words
of my MI5 self-defence instructor,
'Never use karate other than to defend yourself!',
as I stared at the first chap I'd ever enjoyed hitting,
a suddenly sober Miles Manningpot.

The Jester and the new refugee

I met an interesting fellow in the Mountains of Frustration,
that remote but beautiful part of northern England,
who told me he was a court jester,
and proved it with a barrage of jokes and magic tricks,
confessing, 'I like to keep my hand in.'

'You have a look of a chap I met,' he said,
'whose disappearance fascinated the nation,
that of the missing *Match Of The Day* TV presenter, Harry Shootitin.'

'What!' I exclaimed, 'He's my brother.'

Seeing my shock, he declared 'I shall tell you
of the greatest man I ever knew,
who, like me, was condemned as a fool.

'People say I am a silly man, so I am left alone at my
refuge high in the peaks at the rock pool.

'But one day my seclusion was broken by a depressed TV celebrity seeking
solace.

'He was so stressed I couldn't get a word out of him,
but he came to life after my magical pet curlew sang its mating call.

'He told me how as a child, eating his dinner, his mother would
tell him off for dribbling – then he made a fortune doing it with a ball.

'Now people pay to hear him, while they quaff £100 bottles of wine.

'But one day, listening to a member of Parliament,
the much-loved star got into trouble for speaking his mind.

'You see,' he almost sobbed, 'I suddenly had a Damascene moment,
and was compelled to speak out, from the inner depths of my soul.'

'I'd reconnected with it – apparently it was on some social media platform.'

Impressed I said, 'Your brother talked with pride of his working-class fandom,
who loved him as a player but noted a reluctance to pass,
which might have been a metaphor for his current predicament,
and suddenly the conversational floodgates opened,
and how time passed.'

Curious, I asked him 'Do they still follow you?'

'But he replied, looking shamefaced, 'Who, the fans?
No, they can't afford it.'

'Then he talked about his boyhood, running up the
fells around the village of Mechanfaackit,
where he felt really at home, which he never did in
front of the cameras and adoring footie fans,
and now he longed to return to the solace
he'd found on those hilly runs.

'I discovered I'd something in common with my new pal.
For we were both out of fashion, he for annoying the 'yes men' at The Beeb,
and I with my out-of-date comedy act comprising slapstick and silly puns.

'So, I decided to help him cheat the circling pack of reporters,
who had to report that the tabloid press' new object
of scorn had disappeared.'

Well, you can appreciate that I was dumbfounded
by the arrival of this chap.

'What happened next,' I nervously enquired.

'My mountain pool was disturbed by the circling media pack.'

'They were hot on your brother's trail,
but found only leaping frogs,
practising a card trick, involving the Ace of Hearts and the Joker.

'They looked high and low for the missing celebrity,
your so talented but disturbed brother.
But if they'd visited those little music festivals
like Cambridge and Cropredy,
and even that vast commercial enterprise, Glastonbury,
would have found him with me, his new friend the jester,
under the guise of a theatrical ensemble called Hocus Pocus.

'When the reporters returned empty handed,
all they could plead was 'That *Match Of The Week* guy's gone.

'They'll have to replace him with Becks,
on tonight's *Football Focus*.'

‘But old age slows even the fittest,
and our act eventually retired,
with the older man bidding farewell to his sidekick,
who vowed he’d return some day to the jester’s rocky pool.

‘The following day the jestful fellow received a letter saying,
‘I’ve left my homeland seeking refuge from intolerance,
so now I’m no longer regarded as ‘cool’.

‘I never meant to offend, and didn’t even know
how to spell ‘political correctness’.

But I’m now one of those I spoke up for – a refugee.’

‘The envelope contained a newspaper article by a tabloid columnist,
who’d written, ‘The sea is full of them, like an invading army,
as far as the eye can see.’

Dolores the Diva

On a trip to Africa, hunting a 'scoop', I investigated a so-called saintly woman,
regarded by her parishioners as 'Marvellous' Mary, who'd left a comfortable
life in the USA to join a monk called Proinsias at his charitable institute.

Her sponsors, a conservationist called Bashful Brook and the US president,
Harold Calhoun, accompanied by his accountant,
Murgatroyd 'Money Mad' Macroon, would visit every year without fail,
and in her cups Mary would mutter about 'blackmail'.

So, after gaining an audience with her mentor – the above
mentioned monk — I heard him tell his 'disciple' Dolores' 'true' story,
and discovered my subject was not entirely
worthy of praise – in fact her story of innocence stunk,
but I also learned that God truly does work in mysterious ways.

MANY YEARS AGO:
A young woman collapsed from exhaustion,
wishing she hadn't come to Africa,
then, as if moved by miraculous inspiration,
stood up and sang *Abide With Me*,
her grandmother's favourite.

'If only I'd heeded Larry, my childhood sweetheart,
who scoffed at my ambition to be an erotic actress in an arty film,'
mused the distressed traveller,
'he warned me about consorting with that director
who promised he could get me a bit part – I ended up
baring my bottom in a cold studio in Fulham.

'Then there was the deep sea diver 'Shine with Brine' Sangstein,
whom I met in my role as a singer on a cruise liner.'

'It was too tempting to be near so much wealth,
so I jumped ship in Cape Town with a pocketful of jewels.

'Oh my God, my *Bible*-reading gran said I would harness the wages of sin.'

Suddenly a voice boomed out of the heat haze, 'Greetings my dear, you look done in.'

She looked up to see a tall, acerbic monk, who said,
'Hello, I'm Brother Pronsias.
I'd have gone past if I hadn't heard you singing my favourite hymn.'

But years later she reflected that she owed everything
to the man of God who'd saved her life
and provided a safe refuge among the Undopa Mountains,
where she'd kept the monks enthralled with a tale of a
hapless maiden who'd escaped from poverty in Liverpool.

Now a celebrity author, with titles as diverse as *Sizzling Susan*
(the reporter who took on The Mob),
she was invited to a charity event where the guests
shouted 'Sing that Irish song,
I'll Take You Home Again Kathleen!'

Singing with gusto, she was joined by Republican Senator 'Hot Air' Calhoun,
who was running for president, and lauded as a great explorer,
famous for flying his balloon.

But Kathleen had hardly reached home when a voice
she thought had been silenced long ago boomed,
'That song's so corny, didn't I teach you *Molly Malone*?

'Though it doesn't have such a good chorus.

'What's the matter, don't you want to know a lowly holy man now you're famous?'

But in her desire to get away, she tripped over her dress and squirmed
when asked, 'What's the answer, Mary?

'Or should I call you Dirty Dolores?'

Then back in her luxurious apartment, she sobbed,
'I looked like a right idiot falling on my arse.

'I thought he was dead from cholera,

curse that bloody monk, Proinsias.'

But at that moment the man himself was knocking on her door demanding entrance.

As he sat in her room, Brother Proinsias, remembered the heart-rending tale heard he'd heard, 20 years ago,
and suspected she'd told him just what he wanted to hear,
him being a naive young monk, hampered by the innocence of youth.

He was now looking forward to hearing the truth.

PART TWO:
Mary speaks: 'I ended up in Cape Town after a misunderstanding
with the cruise ship's detective, so to escape the cops teamed up with a travelling circus playing my ukulele,
but the owner said he needed something more exotic.

'So I suggested emulating Funny Fanny Fortitude, the Vaginal Magician,
a star turn in the Spanish resort of Benidorm – where I was taken by a guy claiming to be a fashion designer who'd promised me top billing in his next catalogue – it turned out he was married to a clothes salesman from Bradford, whose wife caught us having a snog .

'Where was I? Oh yes, Fanny taught me the trick of
pulling miscellaneous items out of my whatsit.

'So I advertised myself as Dirty Dolores, which certainly attracted the curious.

'The local 'Christians' objected, but fortunately my act had interested leading artist Eustace Horbright who, when I was charged with indecency,
offered a substantial sum for my bail, then asked me to model sans-clothes.

'I agreed, thinking it was better than being in jail.

'I posed in his plush house for hours getting very stiff,
but after a glance in the mirror revealed
that's what he was becoming, I climbed out of a window to
find my way blocked by a guard dog,
but confused him by diving into the swimming pool.

'Dolores paused to gauge the brother's reaction to this,
but Pronsias reflected that this young lady
had inherited the gift of the gab from her Irish grandmother Gypsy O'Toole,
and commented 'He sounds like a right villain.'

Dolores continued, 'I emerged from the water, grabbed a
vine and climbed over the wall,
but not before the canine had fastened its teeth on my arse.

'Oh, excuse my language!'

'I served in the British Army,' answered Brother Pronsias,
'I'm used to the fruity epithets of what a famous general called the licentious soldiery.'

'Oh, you mean Lord Wellington?'

'Indeed, what happened then?'

'I panicked as I heard the cough of an angry lion, so jumped onto a branch.'

At which my sceptical listener asked, 'Aren't you gilding the lily?'

'You may think so, but it was a feat I performed in Michael O'Malley's
Travelling Circus as his famous Leaping Leprechaun.'

The monk snorted, 'Sounds like a lot of old Blarney.'

'Then I ascended a huge tree, and to my surprise heard
the words, 'Hi, want a ride?'

'I looked up to see a cigar-smoking man waving at me from a hot-air balloon,
who said, 'Hang on, while I slow our ascent.

'I can't understand your accent, is that a rare form of Zulu?'

'Then I was hit by a falling sandbag, and woke to find myself
speeding through the air in a wicker basket, desperately needing the loo.

'Where do you do the necessary in a balloon?'
I enquired, 'I need to powder my nose.'

He just laughed, ‘You have a lovely schnozzle.’

'No, it’s an English expression meaning answering a call of nature.’

‘Ah, that explains your accent,’ he said,
breathing whiskey fumes over me, while fondling a bottle.

‘Let me introduce myself – Harry Calhoun.
I’m carrying out a survey of native dialects.’

‘Fascinating, my accent’s called Scouse, from Liverpool,’ I replied.
‘I can give you great research material if you take me to the toilet.
By the way, are you sure you’re fit to pilot this?’

Brother Pronsias leaned back with a frown, commenting,
‘You seem to possess an ability to inveigle your way into
men’s affections so as to advance your cause.’

‘Eh?’ was Dolores’ comment.

‘To put into the vernacular, you’re a bit of a tart.’
At which she rose to slap him, but the brother put her
firmly back in her seat with,
‘I won’t ask what happened next, for I can guess – Calhoun woke
to discover the balloon had gone up,
in more ways than one, as you had nicked his flying machine.’

‘Oh, you know?’‘I remember reading about an explorer who’d reported his
balloon as stolen.

‘Really? Well, I got my just desserts and Harry his flying vehicle,
as he employed a private detective to find me, but ‘Cal’ let me off
when I threatened to accuse him of kidnap,
hinting that I had prior experience of blackmail.

‘My desperate plight forced me into the hands of my old pal,
deep sea diver ‘Shine with Brine’ Sangstein,
who employed me as a pretend mermaid at his
Bizarre Creatures Of The World holiday camp,
until one day I found his hand inside my tail...

'Hang on,' she pleaded, 'I need a comfort break.'

In the bathroom she felt anything but comfortable,
and wondered how to get rid of the elderly cleric,
who, when she returned, asked her, 'So what happened,
did you escape on a passing yacht?'

'How did you know, are you psychic?'

'Well, I did and was nursed by a handsome sailor
who claimed he was a conservationist,
and being a nervous type I became quite sea sick.

'So you appreciated the care he gave you?'
The cleric enquired, with a straight face.

'Indeed, he had a great bedroom manner.'

'Well, I know what happened next, for after he spurned your advances you
jumped ship with a valuable pearl he intended to give his wife,
which he'd found on a coral reef.'

'What!'

Just then the door opened, which saved her blushes,
and to her astonishment in walked her celebrity singing partner,
Senator Calhoun.

'Remember me now?
I rescued you from a nasty situation in my balloon.'

'And if you try and besmirch my name, as I am now officially
a born-again Christian – the voters love that – I and my spiritual advisor,'
and he nodded at the old monk, 'will reveal your shady past,
you seductress and liar.'

The old monk piped up, 'Don't forget to add thief!'

'Indeed,' he agreed, 'and I dread to think
what sinful activities you'll indulge in next.'

‘I’m told you’ve arranged a publicity stunt with an upcoming
British band from your home city, called The Insects.’

At this Pronsias coughed politely, ‘It’s the Beatles.’

‘Of course... anyway, as I was saying, it won’t look good
when you sing along to *Love, Love Me Do*,
when we all know that the only
one you ever loved was yourself, Dolores,
the mischievous madame from Liverpool.’

‘Oh dear,’ she thought, ‘why didn’t I settle for a dull life,
with a husband who drank beer and watched football,
instead of dreaming of fame?

‘Oh, I’m a right fool.’

Just then in walked the yachting conservationist,
with his wife, who asked with a smile, ‘Hi there, old girl.’

‘Can I have my pearl?’

Little Dan

Grandad Flanagan sat on his stool to tell the children a tale he called, 'Where there's a walrus there is a way'.

'Young Dan from Ireland's lovely Dingle was always in trouble at school.
But it all changed when he found Wally, an amphibian mammal,
who, due to pollution, wouldn't enter Mallybotton bay,
and so found herself in some distress.

But a cruising dolphin asked a seagull to fetch Dan,
who'd been studying *Macmillan's Guide to Sea Life*,
and learned that the Atlantic coast was a really good place,
to spot dolphins and their cousins, the porpoise.

His discovery of a sea mammal caused such a stir,
that BBC reporter Molly McMenamaid knew she had to interview him,
but was obliged to take along a well-known comical celebrity,
some fellow called Paly or Palin, who had a lot of influence at the Beeb.

But down south, Dan's uncle,
John Ponsonby-McStickerrick – he had a double-barrelled name
because his mum married a British officer,
during the War of Independence – worried about what
would come out of the lad's mouth, said,
'Sure, the wee lad's a right little gurrier,
making up stories about whales, porpoises and dolphins,
and besides, he's got a stutter.'

But his granny replied, 'Ah, but he has a fine voice.
I always thought he should be a priest,
but he'd have trouble with the sermons.'

But the cuddly sea mammal growled and threw fish at the film crew,
who asked Dan to intervene, due to the special rapport they enjoyed.

When he sang the walrus stopped its growling,
whistling through its big teeth, a tune that,
according to folk-music expert, Máiré Muckrickle,
resembled one by famous blind Irish harpist O'Carolan.

It was heard as far away as that island called Tahiti, in the Pacific,
with dolphins leaping in the air, performing an ancient Celtic dance.

When Dan was informed of this, he said,
'That's where Captain Bligh took the mutinous HMS Bounty,
and then his sailors forced him to leave the ship.'

His granny said, 'God save us, the wee lad's always reading.
He lives in a world of cowboys, pirates and his favourite Red Indian,
Chief Sit-Upon-The-Fence.'

'Don't let him watch a western about General Custer.
He'll tell you what really happened at the battle of The Little Big Horn,
and lament how that Irishman, Captain Benteen,
was blamed for the great disaster that befell the Seventh Cavalry.'

Next morning Dan went for a swim,
a daily exercise to develop his lungs,
as instructed by his doctor, 'Stethoscope' Sean,
who'd encouraged him to take up athletics,
particularly cross-country running.

He fondly remembered how he'd saved the old chap's life,
after he'd fallen while climbing a mountain
range known as The MacGillycuddy Reeks,
and he'd raced away to fetch the rescue team.

Resting on the beach, drifting off into a mindfulness session,
a new fad his big sister had told him calms the channels in the
brain which controls speech, he heard a voice call, 'Let me out!'

Upturning his shoe, he saw a crab which leaped into the arms of an octopus.
They both waved at him before disappearing, and he mused,

'I seem to attract a variety of sea creatures,'
remembering what Gypsy Mary had forecast –

'One day you'll meet a big cuddly animal,
and it will cure you of your impediment.'

So, he slipped into the bay where Wally was slumbering.
'Wake up,' he whispered.
Just then a familiar shape appeared, festooned with a camera,
and he recognised his pal, Snapalot Sinead.

'Jasus, Dan,' she moaned, 'I hope this is worth it.'

Just then Odobenus Rosmarus, the Latin name for Wallies,
which Dan loved to quote, to the amusement of his peers,
eyed the young lad, saying 'Hey kid, I've got a great idea to boost tourism.

'You can jump on my back and we'll sail into the
bay while you recite the *Wild Swans at Coole,* WB Yeats' great poem,
in front of that BBC fellow Paleskin,
or whatever he's called – I did a sketch with when he was
a python you know – while I comb my fading whiskers
and wave a can of hair restorer donated by John McMonagle –
who runs a stall behind Flanagan's bar where I go to sup thrown-away
Guinness.'

'So, you were on the BBC?' asked a starry-eyed Dan.

'Yes, I remember the producer wouldn't give me a fee,
and called me a 'right wally', blaming cutbacks.
So what else is new?

'But Michael said if our paths ever crossed he'd do me a good turn.'

So away they went, causing such a sensation that
the owner of the village hotel thought he could claim this
creature as their own monster,
just like a hotelier is supposed to have done at that Scottish place, Loch Ness.

'Isn't that young Dan, the kid with the stutter?' Asked his missus.

'It's a stammer,' said their daughter, Marianne.

'I heard that Palin fellow – you know,
the well-travelled comic who found a snake called a Monty Python,
on one of his travels for the BBC? – talk about his da,
who was a general practitioner.'

'You mean a GP?' Asked his ma.

'And here he is, Michael I mean, not his da,'
said his other female offspring, Sinead,
'bringing Dan to have his picture taken.'

'Hang on! She cried, 'where's the walrus?'

'The lad swam away,' announced Mr Palin, 'but we've got enough footage.

'He was scared the health and safety people would net him,
and he'd end up in a zoo, eating supermarket out-of-date rotting fish.'

'Now then children,' said Grandad Flanagan,
'if this story had taken place when I was a kid,
young Dan wouldn't go on to become a famous comedian,
like Frankie Howerd, who, as a young man had an impediment, just him.'

Then a girl jumped up, declaring, 'So did singer Ed Sheeran,
actor Samuel L Jackson and politician Joe Biden,' adding,
'But, according to social media, which,
as we all know has replaced reality,
nowadays the political correction police
would condemn Frankie's humour.'

'Yes,' the old man replied, 'but in the old
days youngsters – like that famous Irish comic,
David Allen – who was successful on the BBC,
until he let slip the F word – would listen to auld ones like me,
and thus created a personal,
but unique Irish comical style.'

Then in walked in a nurse, who, being prim and proper,
called patients by their full Christian name,
and exclaimed, 'Oh, there you are, Daniel!'

She was followed by the landlord of O'Malleys pub,
who said, 'Grandad, you old rascal, give us back the stool!'

What makes us human?

Well do I recall the day my wife and I visited a bar
called The Misfiring Musket,
nestling on the banks of Ireland's river Boyne.

I, being a leading literati in the world of fictional adventure, groaned,
when at every alcoholic pit stop, she would boast about my latest comedy,
Love On The Little Big Horn, about a couple obsessed with General Custer
and his demise at that battle of the same name.

It was a military encounter described by historians as
little more than a skirmish,
yet portrayed by Hollywood in martial tones.
But am I much better than those ignorant movie moguls, I wondered,
with my near factory-output of literary trash?

As the wife prattled on, buttonholing the cook and asking
for a recipe for his lovely sausage and mash,
I reflected that the battle which took place barely
a stone's throw away from this little pub,
bedecked with battlefield relics, has been lauded by
some as history-making, maybe even deserving of a Hollywood epic.

Then my eye caught a faded painting, reputed to be several centuries old,
depicting an interplanetary visitor, with the caption,
'A much maligned prophet, and a visitor we should have made welcome.'

Intrigued, I asked a fellow drinker about this – professor James McDaddle,
supping ale with BBC radio presenter Jeremiah Grapevine,
who had been invited there to launch his new radio feature,
What Makes Us Human.

The answer intrigued me, 'It refers to a female from another universe,
who came here in the middle of a battle.

'The one fought between the protestant William of Orange and his catholic rival, King James.'

He laughed, 'Apparently even this famed interplanetary visitor
couldn't bring these two sides together,
and was snubbed by military chiefs who had power
in a land whose motto is 'One hundred thousand welcomes'.

'Instead, we had to wait for the arrival of that very immoral president Bill Clinton!'

'Maybe this female from another world knew something about humanity,
and should have been welcomed,' said a young woman who sprang up,
and introduced herself as Theresa Toogood,
sporting a badge proclaiming 'Jesus Saves'.

The prof asked her opinion, only for us all to be regaled with tales of first-century ancestors who'd fought off Roman invaders,
in a bloody carnage that disfigured her beautiful land.

Until one, a kilt-wearing woman warrior called Mary Littleluv,
appeared out of the mist swirling around the mountain known as Helvellyn.

Natives always claimed she appeared out of nowhere,
but autocratic bishops later claimed they must have misheard,
and she came from the celestial domain of Heaven.

This scary female then encouraged the warlike Cumbrians
to turn away from the path of violence,
and helped them in this aim by falling in love with an enemy,
centurion Marcus O'Reliuss.

Ancient parchment discovered in the Roman settlement of Hardknott
– reputedly written by this military leader – is said to have declared
that his wife was 'Out of this world'.

Laughing about this story, Theresa said, 'My mother always claimed
I bore a resemblance to drawings of the warrior woman,
and as a child I was known as a strange girl.'

After regaling us with this snippet of ancient history and refreshing herself with a glass of stout, which I'd provided at the cost of a stern
look from the wife, she implored us all to, 'Be born again into
the arms of Jesus, and so bring a lasting peace to their troubled land'.

This forthright lady told us about her village of Muttleforce,
in the English county of Cumbria.

But the missus, a confirmed atheist, scoffed at her claim that
humanity could only be defined if we were 'born again',
in a Christian way of course.

Listening to all this was a fellow called Timothy O'Farrell,
who joked that he didn't fancy going through childbirth a second time.

Though being very handsome, Tim didn't half curse,
but she put up with it believing he was destined for fame.

After chiding him for swearing, he laughed, 'I was educated by the Jesuits,
who swore like troopers.'

Later I made notes for my next story: 'Interesting characters – a lady who professes a link to a pagan warrior, and a young actor who I'm sure is destined for stardom.'

Hearing she was accompanying her acting buddy to Hollywood,
I was determined to keep tabs on them, somehow believing our paths would cross.

Sure enough, after my return to that place of moving pictures,
where I, as a writer, was much lauded, I heard a familiar voice shout,
'Repent and you will be saved, for in this town of make-believe,
there is only one star – Jesus Christ.'

Some journalist in the know shouted, 'Your boyfriend's an upcoming film star!'

'Yes,' she laughed, 'but I'm working on him.'

It was her, that lady from Belfast sermonising by a statue of Abraham Lincoln,
the president whom history records as having freed the enslaved.

I wondered, was there some thread in these random events,
that led this lady and the handsome actor here, far from her English village?

My next glimpse of them was while researching a novel,
The Cavalry Man Who lost His Spurs, a sequel to *Love On The Little Big Horn,*
which brought me to the General Custer,
a 'redneck' bar in the US state of South Dakota,
where I was surrounded by arrows, rifles and make-believe scalps,
that, according to the tourist blurb, were from the Indian wars.

History records that one actor in this wild west adventure didn't follow the script – an Indian called Crazy Horse who outfoxed the pride of Custer's Seventh Cavalry, at a battle above that sparkling little stream called the Little Big Horn.

I was wondering how this little woman would cope with this rowdy crowd, but she quietened them with her most stirring sermon, and everyone applauded the little evangelist.

'That's the best speech I've heard since I saw that president address Congress,' commented one old timer.

'What was he called? Oh yes, Abraham Lincoln.'

Then her actor beau O'Farrell piped up, 'I was in that film.'

'What's your next role?' Asked the curious chap.

'I'm playing a soldier in the US 7th Cavalry who follows
an officer who led his men with reckless abandonment.'

'Oh, you don't mean the one whom this bar is named after?'

'Indeed, the movie depicts him as a vain-glorious fool,
unfit to be regarded as a 'Great American hero' by the people of this state,
because he foolishly led his men towards a huge Indian Encampment.'

At this the drinkers turned nasty and we were run out of town in a hand cart,

to be rescued by an ethnoarchaeological expedition,
which had just discovered a cave painting depicting a fabled woman warrior,
known as the Saviour Of The Sioux.

Theresa was astounded by a resemblance between it
and those found in her native Cumbria,
and I noticed a marked resemblance to the painting
I'd seen in that bar by the river Boyne.

A year later I attended the premiere of a film,
May The Muttleforce Be With You,
in which a female hero arrived on earth after
an argument with Luke Skywalker, who apparently was a 'spoilt brat'.

Learning of this the producers of a well-known movie franchise,
the one about wars between stars, threatened legal action.
Timothy O'Farrell, one of the cast of this independent flick,
made by Born Again productions, said,
'I saw enough of that in Hollywood, warring stars I mean.'

He added that the film was funded by a cooperative
bank called Save With Jesus.

Of course, the occasion wouldn't have been complete
without the presence of those two clever chaps I'd met in that Irish bar,
The Misfiring Musket.

Timothy quipped, 'We were going to call the movie
What Makes Us Human,
but couldn't agree on a definition of it.'

Boris visits Yeats Country

My motor car crept along, under the majestic shape of
Co. Sligo's prominent mountain,
Ben Bulben, covered in an ominous black cloud,
as me and the wife explored Yeats' Country.

We filled up at Betty Hanharan's, with a huge pot of tea to follow,
where we met an old chap called Brian,
whose delight it was to visit such a splendid county.

'I'll buy you a glass of stout,' he told us, 'down the road where
the firebugs float in the fading light.'

As we strolled along the strand, I wondered, where had I met him before?
Was it at a dance in a barn?

Then he told us he'd played melodion in an English country band,
during his time in our disunited kingdom.

He even dabbled on the cello, with emerging pop band The Eclectic Late Orchestra.

Then to my surprise, he mentioned seeing Boris Johnson.
'Mr Fixit' himself, cycling through my favourite part of
his former London mayoral domain, Camden.

He told us, 'I used to play in London's Cecil Sharp House, the home of English folk song, and the punters loved my button accordion.'

'Folk music icons Sandy Denny, Swarb and Ashley Hutchings visited there,
unearthing songs of these islands from its library of sheet music,
ballads telling of sailors battling stormy seas,
maidens looking for their maidenhead,
and soldiers fighting for Britain against Napoleon.

'But who's heard of them? 'Instead, the radio waves are full of great,
but commercial artistes, like The Beatles, Stones and Elton.'

Then a storm hit, the wind making a sound not unlike a Scottish bagpipe,
or indeed, the Irish version, with the tongue-twisting name of uilleann.

'It sounds like *O'Carolan's Ode to Sligo*,' our acquaintance informed us,
'you know, he was a famous blind harper, although the notes
seem to be in C sharp; but let's go, the wind's getting stronger.'

As we were hurrying, a huge black cloud appeared above,
and our new pal looked pale as he saw a vision resembling a man called Johnson.

A guy in Hanharan's bar commented, 'Sure, old Boris has lost his charm,
and the English have kicked him out.'

Another quipped, 'Sure, every cloud has a silver-haired former prime minister,
and for him, I'm told, some in the British political elite are still pining.'

The next day our friend informed us he'd had a vision in the night.

It was of former politician Boris, who sternly reminded
him that he would often, after a hard day as London mayor,
sneak into Cecil Sharp House,
and hear the musicians sing and play.

And can he join him in Hanrahans for a pint of stout?

'I've stopped flogging myself as a Winston Churchill expert,' he declared,
'and am now embracing that great poet, William Butler Yeats,
now that I've got Brexit done.

'I love his poem, *The Wild Swans At Coole.*

'Maybe the Taoiseach will welcome me, having forgotten
all the fuss about the Northern Ireland Protocol.'

'A man with a cause is left adrift nowadays,' said Brian, 'as we're all European.'

Then added, 'You're welcome in Ireland, but you can't resurrect your career here, you know.'

'Thanks,' he replied, 'but don't misunderstand me, Éire belongs in Europe.'

'You're like an old cowboy,' commented Brian,
'chasing the buffalo and Red Indian,
but too old to get your foot in the stirrup.

But his new, famous acquaintance countered,
'I run every day, so I'd look good in a saddle.'

Adding, 'I might join our new King Charles for a game of polo...'

An old fellow at the bar laughed, 'You mean the game played by posh people with their arses in the air, wielding those sticks?'

Brian then interjected, with a frown on his face. 'I haven't seen any security people with you.

'All former PMs have them, or are you a victim of cutbacks?'

'Oh,' Boris replied, looking a bit worried, 'they're incognito.'

Just then an English tourist walked in, who asked for 'Sweet Guinness'.

The barman laughed, 'Do you mean Beamish, sure that's a Cork drink?'

'Oh, it's for my dog, she's a prize poodle.'

Then looking round she shrieked, 'So that's where you are, Tim!

I've been looking all over for you.'

'The lookalike agency called – you know that TV show *10 Out Of 10 Dogs*?

'They want you to have a pretend boxing match with Bud Plank;
he's so good, you'd swear he was Donald Trump.

‘Oh, and there’s been another request from that former prime minister, Boris, to stop impersonating him, especially in Ireland.

You’ve been saying things like, ‘It’s a backward place, full of priests and turf bogs.’

‘You make him look a fool – I know, I laughed too.

‘The Irish still haven’t forgotten he was less than honest, over something called The Protocol.’

That evening the band's lead singer got a laugh after his witty quip, ‘This next song’s by an Englishman, but it’s very good!’

Looking at Tim, he said, ‘It’s by a band called The Who, entitled, *Don’t Get Fooled Again!*’

Brian interjected at this, saying, ‘I knew them, back in the heady days of British pop.’

As we drove home the next day, the black cloud had lifted over Ben Bulben.

A truly Christian daughter

Mary Delahinch was often seen with Pappeety,
her short-haired, long-legged Patterdale terrier who,
possessed of a powerful nose, was sometimes used by Colonel
Buntingdon-Blythe to discover a rebel band's hidden gunpowder.

For this cruel man knew her secret – that she was the illegitimate
daughter of Fletcher Christian, the notorious mutineer,
hunted on the high seas after he'd left his tyrannical captain,
William Bligh to navigate a vast ocean with just a compass and sail.

The colonel learned of this through disgraced doctor, Theosephus Tucklady-
Tallimeed, who, though discharged from His Majesty's navy through
drunkenness, not to mention his obsessive pestering of the Admiralty
with his eccentric ideas – such as sneaking up on an enemy frigate
under gas-discharging seaweed – had gained a reputation as a crazy inventor.

So, seeing an opportunity to profit through blackmail,
Theo told the military man that this well-spoken lady was not,
as everyone believed, the orphaned offspring of a Dublin merchant,
who'd died on a voyage home from Spain, leaving her his country estate,
but was born, as the old folk say, on the 'wrong side of the blanket'.

Mary hated letting Pappeete be used to sniff out 'These Fenian devils',
as her uncle called them.

So to annoy her dour-faced relative she flirted
with one of these 'dastardly' rebels,
and, when asked why, declared, 'For a penny bet.'

'Is that all?'

She looked at him with a smile. 'Well, I did get a kiss from Michael McDevitt.'

But her uncle's reply, 'If I were a young man, I'd leather your arse!', was met with a girlish laugh, 'Funny, that's what Michael said he'd do if I tell anyone!'

Then Mary said in a mock, Mayo accent, 'He did say I have a lovely...' But her uncle had walked off with a curse.

Mick was to Mary's aristocratic neighbours a thief and scoundrel – but the downtrodden peasants saw him as their hero.

He ran the yeomanry ragged, planting false trails all over county Mayo, but unknown to him, was being observed through his telescope by Tucklady-Tallimeed, eager to gain a substantial reward.

Michael was drinking with Padraig, Buntingdon-Blythe's gamekeeper, hoping to learn how the authorities had foiled his plans.

But all he discovered was that his childhood-love was learning Irish and playing Gaelic football, delighting in the fact that, unlike the English game of rugby, you were allowed to make a forward pass.

She even tried to take up the game, but was derided by those who belonged to what her uncle would call the lower class.

So she set Pappeety on the trail of an old fox, in Billybruggan woods, to her the epitome of the mythical Reynardine, a fox-like creature who, according to a mediaeval ballad, inhabited the forests of Britain.

Sure enough, the little sniffer led her to a nest of vixen, their mother a victim to the colonel's hounds.
So Mary reared them in the woods, singing Gaelic songs to irritate the military men, as well Rabbi Burns' *My Love Is Like A Red Red Rose,* and *Sir Patrick Spens*.

But one fateful day a dishevelled figure appeared and sang, *A Man's A Man For All That.*

She looked round to see her childhood love Michael, saying, in a breathless voice, 'Oh, that's my favourite of Rabbi's.'

'Nice to know,' he whispered. 'But shift yourself, the hounds are after me!'

Then after she whispered in her terrier's ear, Pappeety sped off,
and they heard the call, 'That way!'

Taking advantage of the diversion they made for Ballyboggan Bay,
where they found the terrier, whose nostrils had guided him to his mistress.
Boarding a French merchantmen headed for the Americas they,
due to storms and a drink-sodden captain, landed on Tahiti,
to be greeted by an old man who introduced himself as Fletcher Christian.

'I've brought you some vixen as a present,' she declared to the delighted chap,
'and Pappeety, a short-haired, long-legged Patterdale terrier.'

'Oh great, I can use the former to outfox my enemies and the latter to find my spectacles, which I leave all over the island.'

Then his daughter became serious, 'But how did you escape the navy?'

'In my youth I dived for jewels buried in the coral, and so can lie submerged on a shoal reef.'

Looking at her, he said, 'I'm sorry I abandoned you, but Captain Bligh forced me to give you up.'

'Oh, if you hadn't have done that I wouldn't have met my love, Michael.
Hang on, he's just fetching the coconut milk, and we'll have some tea.'

Fletcher asked, 'Is he a decent cove, maybe a gentleman?'

'No, he's a rebel, a liar and a thief.'

'Good, I've had enough of gentlemen, he should fit in
with my band of daft mutineers,
who have joined me on my island retreat,
because every island they chose as a hideout turned out to be volcanic.

'Oh, has your intended any medical training?
We're badly in need of a doctor of physick.'

Then, out of the surf rose a figure, bedecked in coconut shells,
that appeared to form some sort of breathing apparatus.

A shocked Fletcher cried, 'Why, I recognise that hollow-cheeked face.
Oh, what's that smell?'

It was his former naval colleague, Tucklady-Tallimeed,
whom he'd left with captain Bligh, who declared, 'I followed you unnoticed,
hidden by my gas-discharging seaweed, whose noxious fumes discouraged
close attention.

Using my network of fellow cast-ashore sailors and ladies of ill repute,
'I was able to discover your expected landfalls at every port.

'But I won't be surprised if you reject me, for I am that traitor who forced you
to flee back in county Mayo.

'On a previous voyage to this place I met my love,
a native called Mannapapatee,
who stopped me drinking – well, she did enjoy a drop
of coconut brandy herself, and we got on like a
house on fire – until I was dragged away by Captain Bligh.'

At this Michael and Mary said, 'Welcome to our new home, we forgive you.'

Now dear reader, you may find this tale to be allegorical,
but Tahitian elders see it is a valuable lesson for children,
who in these days of conformity and the need to be 'cool',
learn that it's okay to rebel.

Indeed, tourists often refresh themselves at the HMS O'Bounty,
an Irish bar with a difference – where there's no shillelaghs,
pictures of the old bog road or anything to do with rebellion.

But the ghost of a short-haired, long-legged Patterdale terrier
sits in the corner with a pair of 18th century spectacles,
waiting for the spirits of Mary Delahinch, Michael McDevitt and Fletcher
Christian.

A father for us all

'You've got a bum and a tum now!' Remarked an old flame,
who'd changed her profession from social worker to children's magician.

'You might be greyer of hair,' she said with a wink,
'but I remember when you were as thin as a lath,
and though your raggedy existence has aged you somewhat,
you're now strong, like a put-out-to-grass ox,
if you'll forgive my back-handed compliment.'

She laughed, did this former refugee gypsy girl from Bosnia Heznovogia,
then, noticing my stiff calf muscles, massaged my anterior ligament.

I'd hurt myself while riding an ostrich in South Africa,
but ironically, the week before in Durban city,
I'd escaped without a scratch after an altercation
with knife-wielding assailants in a public toilet.

So when that flightless bird ran off, I'd toppled arse over posterior.

When I told my lady friend about my brush with death, she was sympathetic,
then told stories of war which made my experience pale.

But when I vowed revenge on my assailants, after a glance at
my unmanly body, her laughter rang around the bar.

Her parents had settled in the Irish fishing port of Killybegs,
where, as a young girl, working in a grocery shop,
boatman Fergus Fontflitt saw her juggling potatoes,
while drop-kicking lemons into a sack.

So, he recruited her to his on-board entertainment crew,
along with fiddler Fred and Barney on banjo, playing Irish tunes,

Boolavogue and Macaverty's Retreat From Magherafail,
while my love performed incredible tricks with herring and skate.

But she was shocked to see her captain – whose real name
was Timothy Titmite – break down in tears,
after admitting he'd been a deserter in the war.

'This made me think,' my old love said,
'for you never know people's back story.
They don't always conform to stereotype,
which I discovered after journeying east over the border,
where killers are revered and old military chiefs still talk rot.
when faced with their mistakes of the past,
and I learned that heroes can be those who don't wish to fight.

'I returned feeling an overwhelming sense of peace,
for I'd met a mysterious cleric called Father Hindelbrand,
on top of Belfast's Cave Hill, gazing out to sea.

'Do not give up on this divided island,' he said.
'You came from a war-ravaged country and have made a life here.

'But Orange men, green-tinged activists and old men wearing khaki
are all different colours of a rainbow, which always has the last laugh.

'For colours do not define man or woman, and when the heavens
disapprove of their behaviour, they are all equally rained upon.'

I was curious, 'Do you still keep in touch with this wise fellow?'

'That's the strange thing, it seems a priest of that name was murdered in
Sarajevo.'

So, I left my old flame feeling rather chastened.
You see, I realised I'd hardly known her, and wondered about this priest.

For I needed someone to restore my faith and, like Christ,
hoped the cleric would resurrect himself.

So, on a whim I popped over to Belfast, where,

on top of that very hill where my old love had stood,
I met a man of the cloth who seemed to know exactly who I was.

Seeing me gaze out to sea, he said, ‘Don’t look east.’

‘Why not?’ I said, startled out of my reverie.

‘There's a border out there in the sea.’

I laughed, ‘Sounds like an Irish joke... Oh, sorry.’

He smiled, ‘I’m not from this little island.’

Then suddenly clapping his hands, he cried,
'It's time to dispel this mood, which has come over me like a deathly pall.

'I shall take you to a bar which I’ve just bought, it’s called A Glass Half Full.'

Walking together I asked him, ‘Where are you from then?’

‘Oh, places where I’ve seen armies invade,
and put back the progress which that fellow who was nailed to a cross made.’

Before I could enquire further, he added, ‘I’ve invited your old
flame to do magic tricks for the children, along with a band from Killybegs,
with Fergus Fontflitt to sing vocals, who’ll get us all up to dance.
We might even get your old love to drop-kick lemons into a sack.

‘To finish the evening, we’ll sing that song by a man who
met his end at the barrel of a gun, like so many from this place.
It’s called *Give Peace A Chance.*

‘The guy who wrote it’s from Liverpool, which welcomed emigrants – like me.

‘I believe he had a hit single – I refer, of course, to John Lennon.’

I smiled, ‘Should be great craic.’

‘Yes,’ smiled the cleric; oh, I didn’t get your name.’

'My parents christened me Kevin, after a little-known Irish saint.
It's annoying that everyone celebrates the other chap,
the one who rid this land of snakes, and not my namesake,
even though the snake banisher was born in England.

'That's very true,' he sympathised. 'Pleased to meet you.
I'm Father Hindelbrand.'

In memory of a misanthropic cleric

Did you go to that place of the timorous tiger,
and look in awe in at an elephant with a very long ear,
which, according to legend was faithfully followed by a cow,
mooing in tune to *God Save The Queen,*
that wistful sound echoing across those
mist-covered hills from the army camp?

I asked the spirit of my great-granddad,
regimental Padre Beauchamp,
derided by his family as a 19th century misanthrope?

And did you condemn Lieutenant Lionel Tigworthy-Teague
and his mistress, Millie, who, treading softly though the
jungle hoping for an illicit embrace – disturbed your
daily prayer for friends lost in the Indian Mutiny,
slain in that fight before the ramshackle defences of Cawnpore?

Perhaps, I mused, he wished to reach out to them,
but instead turned away from their congress.

I received no answer of course, yet the cow mooed in sympathy
and the quiet tiger roared, but the elephant simply
nodded a sagacious head,
as I sobbed bitterly in that valley of the slain.

But I was reliably told (by a regimental historian),
that on parade next day my great-grandad, hugging a *Bible*,
had noticed the lieutenant's scorn-filled glance at him,
as he jumped while conducting morning service,

startled when the sergeant reprimanded private Littlefrance,
after he dropped his rifle.

But in his anxiety to remain aloof, as a good misanthrope should,
he ignored the glance from unfaithful mistress Millicent,
clapping her husband Major Bunty-Blowflitt,
bowling a maiden over in the Civil Service versus Army cricket match,
wondering if she knew the padre was aware of her secret,
as he set off on his daily pilgrimage, to again
seek comfort with a tiger and its odd-looking elephantine companion,
taking comfort that he was not the only one regarded as 'queer'.

For being whispered about as a 'poof', while in the service of God,
can turn a military man away from the fife and drum.

Is that why you discarded your holy raiment and joined the road sweepers,
and those other Indian Untouchables whom the soldiers called 'scum?'
I deigned to ask.

But walking along that valley as a 20th-century tourist,
saying a prayer for great-grandfather Beauchamp,
I seemed to spark a friendly roar from the tiger,
but couldn't see that faithful cow following behind its elephantine idol,
or hear its patriotic *God Save The Queen.*

Well, even a devoted pilgrim can change its tune,
I mused, as I gratefully accepted a ride on the back
of the elephant with a long ear,
and imagined that scornful lieutenant and his mistress,
following behind arraigned in native dress,
paying homage to the spirit of a
much-maligned regimental padre.

Here's to you, Mary Lou

'I'm working on my memoirs, dear Mary Lou,
recalling several memorable days spent with yourself,'
I announced, but as usual didn't receive an answer.

Bemused, I thought back to the day it all started,
that day in Dublin waiting for the St Kevin's Bus,
when we both tra la la lallied to a busker who sang,
'*I Met My Love On St Stephens Green*'.

This turned out to be prophetic, because it was in that lovely Dublin park,
surrounded by images of the glorious uprising of 1916,
that I'd first espied her looking at the statue
of that remarkable writer, Samuel Beckett.

'I'm trying to work out who he is,' she said,
pointing at the bust with a puzzled frown,
'isn't he the one who's still waiting for God?'

I laughed, 'I think you mean Godot.'

This interesting lady then announced she was
about to complete a long-awaited pilgrimage,
namely to that lovely vale of Glendalough,
in the county of Wicklow.

When we stopped in Bray she awoke as from a disturbed dream and,
as a posse of Americans filled our omnibus,
hid behind my slender frame.

I wondered what your secret was, Mary Lou – as we
peered into St Kevin's Bed,
the indentation in the cliff inhabited by that ancient hermit,

which towered above the lough's peat-filled depths
in that lovely valley of the glen with two lakes,
the literal meaning of the valley we'd both escaped to.

But as dawn broke the next day we stood amid the
vale's ruined monastic settlement,
and I listened enraptured as you sang,
'Hello, lovely birds of prey', your silky voice seeming to shake a mist-
shrouded round tower, upon which perched a kestrel and an eagle.

'Are you talking to yourself?' I asked.

'Look!' she replied, 'It's Beaky Pete and his girlfriend Kate The Kestrel,'
pointing at the wide-winged birds, the male of which,
she claimed, was taking a break from the Stars And Stripes flag
at Dublin's US embassy.

'Anyway, we better continue with the purpose of our early morning walk,
which is to make a confession to the home of a monk,
to whom my dreams have compelled me to visit,
located in the ruins of this ancient monastery.'

She then gave voice, 'Dear venerable spirit,
please forgive me for following the ways
of that notorious pagan, Laurie Littlehampton-Knox,
although I was brought up a catholic...'

Just then a strong wind blew and I lost the rest,
only to hear, 'This valley's like a wind funnel.'

Looking round I saw a funny little chap,
who introduced himself as Syracuse The Shepherd.
'I'm half-Greek you know,' he announced,
'I came here after the war seeking solitude – in fact,
the locals say the wind blew me in!

'By the way, you know that Knox fellah she mentioned?
He was arrested after rumours about
a cult in the mountains of Idaho.'

'What a funny man,' I said to Mary Lou, but she'd vanished.

But there were two men with bulging jackets,
one muttering in a New York accent, 'The doc thinks she's off on another wander.'

'You see,' the woman herself whispered to me in the Glenvale Hotel,
where I'd tracked her down, hiding behind a menu,
glancing surreptitiously at a man who was saying
he'd seen a face familiar from a television news item,
I listened with notebook in hand, as she declared,
'It was cool to be different in those heady days of drug-filled abandon,
surfing along to those all-American Beach Boys, singing 'Surfin' USA,'
while openly admiring that great rebel Jimmy Hendrix.

'Did you know he jammed with those doyens of English folk-rock,
Fairport Convention, not once but twice?

'Of course,' was my reply, 'I told you, I'm a journalist.'

'Really? Anyway, where was I – yes, I saw them at Knebworth;
I and Bill Clinton hitchhiked there when we were up
(or is it down?) at Oxford.

'But I digress – it's a bad habit, the doctors reckon I took too much cannabis…'

Only for her to be interrupted by a shout of, 'There you are!'
from a chap who turned out to be US Presidential Secretary,
Larry Letterfull.

'I got in so much trouble, he moaned, 'when I lost you at the airport.'

As they walked off I heard him whisper
to a serious-looking individual from the CIA,
'I'm afraid the vice-president's wife is in the early stages of dementia.'

'What's more, Bill – yes, I do mean Clinton – is anxious she doesn't
blurt out what they got up to at some place in England called Knebworth,
listening to those old rockers Led Zeppelin.'

'But what about that Knox fellow, arrested by the FBI?'

‘Oh, he’s old hat, why, half the senate were cult followers!’

Well, as I write this from a secluded hideout,
I am soothed by the voice of Mary Lou,
singing ‘Help, help me Rhonda’,
and I mused, ‘It’s a good thing I like The Beach Boys.’

I’m content in the knowledge that MI6, who,
according to a source at *The Times* are being asked by
the US to serve me an arrest
warrant for kidnap – would not connect the
author Lou Marie with that woman in my cottage,
who’s known to the locals for
talking nonsense while playing with her toys,
and even claims she possesses ‘the gift’.

But she can write brilliantly about Katie
the Kestrel and an eagle called Beaky Pete,
who often flies to the lovely vale of Glendalough,
leaving his post on Uncle Sam’s flag at the
US Embassy in Dublin.

There he’s fed by a little Greek who,
according to ancient cave drawings,
closely resembles that other mysterious hermit, St Kevin.

False teeth distort the truth

As a young man I visited Galway on the island of Ireland,
with its massive bay, so famed in song, and set off on a trip
to visit those remote Aran Islands under the tutelage of our guide,
a comedian called Tommy.

He boasted that he would just shut his eyes and 'hope for the best',
while driving a coach which seemed to hover on the edge of a great precipice.

We all laughed, except some American ladies who,
with their transatlantic humour,
or maybe lack of it, didn't get the joke,
covering their eyes with their hands.

We sailed to the island of Inishman,
with hardly a breeze to worry our passage,
but Madge, an actress from New York,
seeing I was trapped to starboard by Mary MacStew,
a notorious bore, kindly rescued me, but alas,
only at the cost a long diatribe about an old flame,
Miles Manlycamp, whom she'd met while playing
in *The Playgirl Of The Western Swirl,*
a controversial take on JM Synge's homage to male heroism,
Playboy Of The Western World.

But walking along the shore of this tranquil island,
we suddenly stopped to gape at a little fellow climbing up a precipitous cliff,
which rose like a sentinel out of the sea,

The climber then disappeared inside a tiny mediaeval church,
half-sunk beneath the sand.

'You're a fine-looking woman,' commented the curious chap,
on emerging from the narrow confines of that holy place.

He went by the name of Micky Paddermunce, and bore a marked resemblance to the comical driver, Tommy.

'Thank you,' she responded with a blush, 'Are you connected with this building?'

'God bless you, not at all, I'm looking for my teeth.

'I slept in here last night after drinking too much stout.'

Then he looked at her with a penetrating gaze,
'I'm blessed with the gift of foresight,
and predict you'll have a sparkling career as a novelist.'

Then he wandered off, singing a ballad in Gaelic.
Madge wondered what this meant, and vowed to take up her pen.

Returning to New York she starred in the play, *Funny Girls Have More Fun,*
wearing a glittering dress, to become a much vaunted star on Broadway,
an object of admiration for gay men, as the madame of a house of ill repute,
singing 'My best friend's a ponce,' which 'opened the curtains
on a hidden world of perversion!' according to Glen Beachamp,
the city's celebrated critic.

Her old actor friend Miles remarked, 'Maybe you misheard the
old chap in Ireland, for they do talk peculiar.

'I appeared there in my camp version of *The Quare Fellow,*
that play by Brendan Behan, Dublin's famous rebel.'

Picking up the magazine, *Literally Literature,*
she read a review of her debut novel,
Guardian Of A Holy Relic, inspired by her time in beautiful Erin.
The headline declared, 'By gum! Toothless islander spawns historical tale'.

However, her contentment was soon dampened by rival publication, *Power Of The Pen*, who lambasted Madge's status as a 'serious' writer, in a scathing editorial, 'A woman who shocked the public by playing a fetishist!'

'Ah!' she exclaimed, 'that's what the old chap meant that day on Inishmaan.

'When he took his teeth out – I thought he said 'novelist'!'

A Lancashire Lad Makes Good

I'm a Lancashire lad who raced in spikes and string vest,
a good athlete on the track and cross-country,
but was a disappointment to my old dad,
who'd dreamt of his only son scoring for the Saints,
that iconic rugby team with the red V.

I said it was just as well, 'cos I would surely have
dropped the ball, being all fingers and thumbs.

'But being a clever boy, I went up to Oxford,
where I impressed the athletic club with my running ability,
as well as a certain public school-educated Dorothea Diddle-Dashit,
who loved to scrub me down after I got wet and muddy.

After hearing me play the banjo uke, she invited me to
join her radical folk group, The Berkshire Bums.
I brought her home to meet my grammar-school pals,
and in a typical Lancashire pub, The Winsome Whippet,
we discussed ways of redistributing wealth,
espousing the cause of that radical economist John Maynard Keynes,
and admiration for Beveridge, who improved Britain's National Health.

When malicious tongues accused me of forgetting my roots,
Dorothea said that was 'a lot of rot',
as we shivered in my parents' outside loo,
the only place we could go for privacy,
for my strict mother watched us like a hawk.

I heard later Dot boasted how she'd once done it in a privy!

I won't bore you with the story of my failed romance,
but I smiled through gritted teeth when Dorothea and childhood sweetheart,
Lord Monty Middlechamp, were married.

She tried to console me by fixing me up with her pal Mavis,
who whispered, 'Try not to step on my toes,' during a slow dance.

Feeling like a lost soul I moved to Wigan, where,
while working at Wadsworth's Pickle Pie Emporium,
I invented a revolutionary food additive,
which destroyed an unfortunate side effect of a famous delicacy.

Our chairman, Dashing Dai Daffyd, who'd come north to play
for the town's famous rugby league club,
said, 'This young man has revolutionised our pickle pies.

'When I came here, people said,
'You chaps score lots of tries, and that's why we all love the Welsh.'

'But I didn't like to say, "You should invent odour eaters,
for these pies don't half make you belch.

'Now, thanks to our Oxford graduate I can kiss
the missus and be assured of afters,
when I come home for my tea.'"

This elicited a scathing editorial in *The Times* from Beatrice Bountiful-Bunion,
who wrote, 'Chairman Daffyd sounds like a typical northern fossil,
watching a game played by 'Saints' and 'pie eaters'.'

He should come into the modern world,
leave that northern sport with
its early baths and up-and-unders,
and watch football and rugby union.'

But Dashing Daffyd invited her to watch Wigan versus Hunslet,
and she saw Chariots Of Fire score from his own try line,
which got her thinking, 'This is better than watching scrums that take so long,
one has enough time to powder one's nose and buy a drink.'

Using my fame as the chap who'd made pie eaters acceptable in polite circles,
her agent secured a television advert for us,
with myself eating one of Wadsworth's products,
and Beatrice sweating away at a stereotypical Lancashire kitchen sink.

Rising up the social ladder, her and I were rated,
along with rock-music couple, Nick and Francia Jongleur,
in *Tatler's* magazine's top 10 'cool' couples,
and how my light shone, but inwardly my soul was dying,
like a long-distance walker slowing with fatigue.

You see I was trying to fit in, and following instructions from Beatrice,
said I was from Cheshire, and not St Helens, while sitting in the VIP box at Chelsea FC.

But she gave me a stern look when I whispered, 'Oh, to watch some rugby league!'

I was even roped into doing a televised charity 100-metre dash pitted against a Bond movie villain and a rock guitarist, and I appeared in upcoming Scottish band The Proclaimers pop video,
playing my ukulele, singing a slightly left-of-centre
parody of Bob Dylan's *Million Dollar Bash.*

Then a chap called 'The Voice Of The People', writing in the *Mirror,*
accused me of denying my roots, and I nearly hit the fellow,
when I tracked him down, in his Fleet Street haunt, The Scribbler.

But he bought me a pint and advised I take a reality check,
after I confessed I'd been asked to do another advert,
this time to promote soap,
dressed as a coal-covered miner with hobnailed boots.

My old dad was not impressed, saying I looked 'A right fool',
cosying up to celebrities, by 'playing your banjo uke'.

Then one fateful day, strolling through Hampstead Heath,
who should I see but my old love Dorothea, sitting on a bench looking forlorn.

'Oh darling,' she cried, 'how I've missed you!'

'Isn't married life with a lord suiting you then?' I asked, with a hint of scorn.

'No,' she answered bitterly, 'as soon as we donned our skis he fell on his ass, and had to stay in our hotel for the whole honeymoon.

'I returned one day to find him turning down the sheets
with a chambermaid from Belfast, Mary McAfluke.

'It seems they had a fling at Cambridge, and she was making beds to pay for her PHD!'

Then to my delight, Dorothea exclaimed, 'Take me back to
wherever you're from, wasn't it some town peopled with flat caps and
whippets?

'I jest – but seriously, I know it's some place where rugby players,
unlike my daddy's team, Henley RUFC, form an uncontested scrum.'

'But darling! I cried in an unconvincing voice, 'I'm engaged to Beatrice;
you know, *The Times* columnist.'

'Oh you fool, she's using you to make her look politically correct.
Where is she now, I wonder?'

I looked at Dorothea suspiciously, 'She's covering a
Ski Hotel conference in Biarritz,
listening to boring talks on discount package-holiday deals'

She laughed, 'And guess where my husband is?'

Realising I'd been duped by a scion of the fairer sex,
I cried, 'Oh, we were so happy, under Oxford's dreaming spires
playing music and running across the dew-laden fields.'

Then I listened entranced as she sang Ewan MacColl's
The First Time Ever I Saw Your Face, and I fell in love again,
listening to her falsetto voice.

Next week, tuning into BBC Radio 2's folk music programme,
my old dad gasped when he heard the host, Mark Radcliffe,

interview a band about their new single,
a parody of the Strawbs' hit, *Part Of The Union,*
penned by my good self and wittingly entitled,
You Won't Get Me I'm Part Of The Illusion.

'We sing about real people...' Dorothea, the lead vocalist,
declared, 'We're not a 'cool' indie band, exploring teenage angst.
Rather, we sing about scarlet-coated riders failing to catch a fox,
while maidens dance around a maypole.

'Why, we even turned down an invite to do *Top Of The Pops.*'

'Hang on!' My aged parent shouted at the radio, 'I know that voice.
It's my son's ex, Dorothy or Dorothea, summat like that!'

He listened entranced as she continued, 'All the band have
one thing in common – we don't conform.

'For example, Percy, our bassist prefers men to women...'

At which the aforementioned shouted, 'Last night I was mocked
by a chap with a huge beard, drinking real ale,
who accused me of batting for the other side,
during a rendition of *John Barleycorn.*

'I told him I wasn't like him, a stereotype of English life,
and the audience laughed, even his wife.'

Dorothea laughed, 'Indeed Percy – where was I?
Oh yes, I was too influenced by my jolly hockey-stick chums,
and allowed them to steer me away from Mr Right.

'That's why we're here, with you Mr Radicalstife,
for it is him who suggested we reform The Berkshire Bums...'

The radio host then looked embarrassed as she gazed into my eyes.

'...Then I realised what a resourceful chap my husband is – why,
he used an Oxford degree to invent non-windy meat pies.'

Shortly after me and the missus were celebrating in my dad's local pub,
The Faltering Fullback, when the old chap said to her,
'Welcome to the family.'

'Thanks,' she laughed, then putting on her public-school voice, said,
'I'll have a pint and a Wadsworth's meat pie.'

Soldier Les with the fez

*The following is an extract from a torn and tattered journal,
made by private MacPherson, renowned as a poet,
of the Shropshire light Infantry*

Corporal Lesley Loveday, known to his mates as Laughing Lez,
had such a reputation when in service of the British Army,
he was allowed to wear a fez.

He bought it from a native in a house of ill repute,
who claimed it was blessed by Allah, a claim the squaddie dismissed.

'How could a hat protect me from a spear?' He asked.
'I respect your belief, but I was reared as a devout Methodist.'

Then a boy, the son of a fallen woman,
threw a lance at him which mysteriously
swerved and hit a badmash (or bandit), who was about to slit Les's throat.

He was so shocked and overwhelmed with gratitude,
he felt compelled to rescue the woman and her son,
who praised him for saving them from a house of ill repute.

The fez saw him through a bloody campaign in Afghanistan,
where he stood firm in the infantry square when all about him ran.

But shortly after arriving in the British colony of Natal,
he found himself on a hill in Zululand,
looking down on 1,000s of warriors in King Cetewayo's kraal.

Les returned from his scouting mission,
reporting that the Zulu army was more than 'A bunch of savages',
to quote the generally-held military opinion.

Alas, his warning went unheeded, but though the Zulus
achieved a stunning first victory, the result of the war was never in doubt.

Though he lost many friends, the spears couldn't penetrate his cheery exterior,
and Les earned the Victoria Cross for his part in defending a bloody redoubt.

But, ashamed over his part in the destruction of a proud native people,
he unburdened himself in a brothel to a disgraced mother superior,
and deserted when his regiment returned to Aldershot.

He was often to be seen around Durban, his sanguine face
topped by the battered fez, which the native kids threw stones at.

'Go away!' he grumpily shouted.

But they replied, 'We've been disenfranchised by British imperialism.
We had our human rights, which you so openly flouted.'

He stopped and reluctantly concurred, 'Indeed.
Where did you learn to talk so intellectually?'

'We attended a school run by an Irish nun, Mother Superior Rosin.
She was kicked out for being critical of British policy.

'They didn't like her singing *Revenge For Skibbereen,*
which apparently is an Irish rebel song.'

Les was amazed at this lucidity from those so young.

'Thank you,' they responded to his compliment.
'We are told you fought well in the war,
for Cetewayo's impis were taught well how to fight.

'But we should not be regarded as second-class citizens.
Our only sin is being born black instead of white.'

Les bowed, 'Well, I have met said lady and, though impressed,
was shocked by her admission, that being a catholic she was
not a devotee of the *Bible*.

'But though I was brought up by a Methodist minister,
I had more in common with her than him,
even though her dad was an Irish rebel.'

He paused for breath, 'I haven't talked as much since
I made a speech after knocking out Fists O'Flaherty for
the army featherweight boxing title.

'You have pointed out my sins, of which I am ready to confess.
I have done great wrong to your kind, little Zulu,
so you can have my trusted fez.'

The children danced with glee, and when a certain Irish lady appeared,
they all chorused, 'Hello Rosin!'

Who declared, 'This reminds me of when I was a young nun teaching at the mission.

'But I have left the religious life, and Les, I must ask, can I be your wife?'

The surprised ex-squaddie replied, 'You bet!'

'Great, and If you're worried about my chastity,
I escaped from the knocking shop where we met.
It was my first day, and you were such a gentleman.

'What I am trying to say is, I am still virgo intacto.'

So after marrying, the couple expressed a wish to help
the dispossessed of Zululand.

With the help of warriors loyal to King Cetewayo, they built a hospital-cum orphanage.

Life was tough, but Les used his sharp-shooting skills and ability to forage.
In return she taught him Gaelic history, of Finn McCool
and the scourge of Cromwell, reminding the old soldier that Lord Wellington,
who defeated Bonaparte at Waterloo, was born in Dublin.

‘Indeed he was my love.

'So grab a drop of gin and raise a glass to Lord Wellington, Zulus,
disgraced nuns and rebels of every kind,and damnation to imperialist rhetoric.

‘Throw away our rifles and spears, and let’s shed no more wasted tears.'

Roisin agreed, ‘Oh that’s quite poetic.

'Alas, though our union has not brought forth offspring,
I do have a strong man to comfort me in my dotage,
and I content myself that I am a mother to lots of children,
in our little hospital-cum orphanage.

‘But you are getting a beer belly, dear husband.

So please pay little heed to the call of John Barleycorn,
which is an English allegorical name for beer
(I learned that from a publican).
And due to not marching you are not regular.’

‘Indeed,’ he concurred. ‘John Barleycorn is a well-known ballad.
So to stop your nagging, I’ll go into the garden and pick some salad.’

But as he bent to pick up a lettuce, a voice called, ‘Hello, Mr Les!’

He looked up to see a native, who declared,
‘When I was a boy, you gave me your magical fez,
I believed it would give me a charmed life.

‘Alas, I discovered it only works for imperialist white men,
with rifles versus spears, like against the Zulu.

After all, that war wasn’t like taking on the Russians at Balaclava,
or the French at Waterloo.’

Les lifted his eyebrows. ‘Are you a devotee of Karl Marx?’

'No, just a former pupil of your missus.
By the way, she told me to tell you not to forget the onions,
or you'll be washing the dishes.'

'Oh, thanks for reminding me, you certainly know yours.
By the way, I was at Balaclava and it wasn't a walk in the park.'

The native nodded. 'I respect your courage.
Now apparently, you have become a bit of a journalist.'

Les blushed, 'Since the wife taught me proper grammar
I like to express my views, which may have some influence,
me being a former soldier.'

This elicited a smile, 'Indeed, you have stirred up a
veritable hornet's nest, with your article condemning white rule.

'I think you will need help once the Boers have read the *Durban Bugle*.
So have this with my blessing, and regards to Mrs Les.'

The old soldier beamed at him, and said, 'Why thank you.
It's my lucky fez!'

Postscript

*An article, Victorian Heroes, appeared in the magazine History Makers,
highlighting the story of a deserter, Corporal Lesley Loveday,
known colloquially as Laughing Les with the fez, an awardee of the Victoria Cross.*

*It described his role as a humanitarian in the former British colony of Natal,
and concluded that his name should be reinstated on the roll
of honour of the Shropshire light Infantry.*

The African Animal Protection Symposium

The following is a report by BBC Wildlife
campaigner Sir David Attenborough,
addressing the Royal Society for The Protection of Wildlife

'Contrary to popular belief, the magical ostrich
Awesome Ozzie possesses a large brain,
and is regarded by naturalists as a freak,
helping drought-stricken villages when the clouds refuse to precipitate.

However, he is outdone in that department by Percy The Pop-up Pelican,
who carries gallons of water in its huge beak,
helping drought-stricken people in countries like Ethiopia and The Yemen.

One day these remarkable creatures,
encouraged by their contact with the species human,
decided to establish The African Animal Protection Symposium.

The following is an extract from a report concerning this worthy endeavour,
written in a language used by the animal world, called Flapalongspeak,
in which I am fluent, along with my globetrotting TV colleague,
Michael Palin, he of the genus Monty Python.

This valuable document gives an insight into the tragic
demise of this worthy body,
which never really got off the ground, rather fitting
for an organisation headed by a flightless bird.

The opening statement from Chairman Ozzie, read as thus:

'Despite them hunting tigers and elephants,
I propose we improve relations with the creature known
as the homo sapien – and before we go any further – why are we

having such a big menu, when many of our man friends
exist on fare more frugal?'

The secretary Percy interjected, 'Good question,
can you submit that in a memo?'

To which his winged pal replied, 'Will it be acted upon?'

'Of course,' he replied, 'we're animal, not human.'

Looking down on this expression of discontent was an aged bird,
Edmund The Seagull, a recent arrival to the African continent.

He squawked, 'We need to reflect on the benefits brought by immigrants,
and think of a parallel, if that's the right word,
that mankind has 'emigrated' into our animal world.

'Some of whom would rather have remained in their native land,
but are forced to leave by war and famine,
like the settlers penetrating the North American continent,
with nothing more to protect them than muskets from
wolves and marauding Indian.

'Indeed,' commented the secretary, 'Not to mention the Dutch settlers,
invading the African interior and annoying that warrior nation, the Zulu.'

'Can I interject, Mr Chairman?' Asked Ozzie.

'What about that animal from which the Injuns,
as John Wayne called 'em – got everything from fur coats to protein?

'I refer of course to the mighty Buffalo.'

'Indeed,' the seagull replied, 'our horny friend was decimated by man.

'Now your best chance of seeing one is in a zoo,
rather than an American prairie.'

Edmund flapped his wings, 'Anyway, I'll carry on – I was
brought here by a mighty typhoon,

snatched away while studying philosophy
when I nested on the transparent roof overlooking
the Library of Moral Thought, on the Left Bank in Paris.

'I learned great words, such as allegorical (which I believe this poem is) and schism.

'Gosh, that was a mouthful.
'Now apparently, I enjoy equal status with that crusty old bird,
The Enlightened Eagle, who, due to an unscheduled flight to Burma,
is now a devotee of the religion called Buddhism,
which teaches love and the middle way, and coincidentally,
is the emblem of that huge country, The USA.

'I once landed in *The Bible* Belt there, and am now a Christian.

'But despite this, unlike our so-called human superiors,
whose various creeds have caused wars down the centuries,
we and the Buddhists get along.

'So, to conclude my address – and thank you for inviting me – I hope
there will be many more symposiums where we can talk to those
creatures who soar above, insects which burrow beneath the soil,
fish who populate our oceans, when they are not
being smothered with plastic and oil, and even the whale,
the master of all the genus amphibian,
hunted almost to extinction by that creature who still hasn't
learned not to hate, the homo sapien...'

Chairman Ozzie then wrote:
'It is with great regret that we and my fellow delegates
never got to hear the rest of our colleague's fine words,
as our conference venue, the dark interior of a thorny bush,
was nearly destroyed by a BBC wildlife camera team,
looking for a species called the Greater Grested Worm.

'I could've saved them the trouble, I hadn't seen one for years.

'Anyway I, being an ostrich disillusioned by that species
known as the genus human,

who love to ogle my fellow animals behind the bars of a zoo –
will now, like the former, act according to type and
bury my head in the sand.

'By the way, if you see my pal, Percy, now known as The Pop-Under-Pelican –
he feels safer under water than above it – give him my regards, will you?'

The Spirit Meade

I am interested in the musings of the spirit Meade,
was the random thought that entered my subconscious.

But it was quickly banished to that no-man's land lying between
the front-line trenches of reason and despair,
those two enemies constantly at war.

Gathering all my strength, I pushed it away,
though it would, like a schoolboy exploring London's Soho,
occasionally stray into the lower strata of my mind.

Not the morally authoritarian superego part, you know,
christened by the father of psychology, Sigmund Freud,
but the dark, twisted ID, that eminent psychologist's word
for the place where primitive impulses lurk.

Why do they daily appear, like a repentant penitent
supping the chalice at holy mass?

That's the question I would put to the
all-knowing spirit of Meade,
and what's more, can its celebrated musings really answer
the great imponderables of life?

Answers on a postcard to my hide-out, care of the Mad Monk,
(which is what the staff know me as) care of Kickass Abbey,
now a NHS mental health walkin-in centre --- but don't tell the wife.

Johnson O'Pouncy, the mysterious Englishman

Those who remember that enigmatic fellow, Johnson O'Pouncy,
were told by those who knew him in the old West,
that, though he appeared to be of limited means,
he'd amassed enough funds to take over a shack
just outside Horsetrough City, in Texas,
which wasn't worth a hill of beans.

Neighbour Jebadiah Jenkinson remembers meeting this tall,
enigmatic man with his dog Cactus, and wondering
what he was doing in this arid country.

He claimed to have arrived on an emigrant ship,
bedding down in steerage, the part reserved for the lower class,
amazing the Poles and Russians by conversing in their native tongue,
his fine voice endearing him to the Irish with a great rendition of
Galway Shawl.

He even amused the children by organising a round of 'I Spy'.
When little Johnny asked him why that game, he said,
'Spying is the greatest game of all.'

As a kid he'd dreamt of being a captain on his own bridge,
but the voyage's reality was stark in contrast to his imaginings.

But the air was so fresh on North America's great plains,
and he didn't care that his home turned out to be an
old shack nestling in the shadow of the Black Mountain Ridge,
but to the local women's consternation, never took a wife.

He'd bought the place from old timer, Mocassin Mohawk,
who'd fought the Spanish, but left the Alamo before that Texan fort fell,
leaving his respect for the American way of life,
and its obsession with those rigid values of the old south.

Johnson also became friends with guitarist Senor Montevido,
who's playing delighted his little dog,
a delightful pet who danced fit to bust.

When sheriff Pistol Pete called, the pet had great fun playing with his spurs.

'You can take 'em off you know,' commented Johnson…

'Ah, but wait, you might have to jump on yer 'hoss',
and set off after the Dead Gulch Gang,
like you told that writer from New York, Frederick Fortitude-Forthright,
who featured your daring deeds in that popular rag,
Wild West Wonders under the title, *Tales Of A Texan Lawman*.

At which the sheriff uttered a curse, 'Aw shucks, I needed the money.
Anyway, the readers want escapism, and those dime novelists provide it.
Now, are you going to tell me what a refined chap like you is doing here?'

O'Pouncy looked at him with a frown. 'Ah, the truth at last.
Well, I could tell you I left 'cos I was heartbroken over a woman.
But I'll be honest – I was engaged by Britain's chief spy master,
Chrispin Cockslip, to ensure this state stays on the right side in any conflict.'

'You mean one that's beneficial to The Crown?'

'This land, dear sheriff, is like that fruit cake you see
on my table – full of riches, and my king wants a slice of it.'

Later Johnson reflected on his mission and why he'd revealed it to Pete.
'Am I bound by a promise to my king?' He mused. 'Could I not forget it?'

'Indeed you can,' whispered a spirit which emerged from the night.

'Is that you, Fiona,' He gasped, 'or to give you your full title,
Lady Fiona Fulsome-Fultitude?'

'Indeed it is, my dear Johnson,' the ghostly shape answered,
'I was summoned by the tunes of this great guitarist,
whose Celtic tale reminded me of your crisis of conscience.

'Unlike other invaders of the Emerald Isle, you didn't murder and pillage.

'You refused to burn peasant hovels, after winning a battle,
in that most beautiful county of Ireland, Wicklow.

'And I abandoned you – as unfitting for the daughter of
Lord Billings of Bude – even though you'd encouraged me to ride properly,
unlike those silly madams at my prep school – by keeping my arse in the saddle.

'So I married your colonel, and thus gained the married name of Fulsome-Fultitude.

'You were recruited by a master spy and sent to this land,
which in the words of the Scottish emigrant,
Professor Theodosius Thackaria,

''*Is full of harsh environs, yet boasts nature's gifts,*
enough to feed a mighty multitude.''

'Indeed,' concurred her former lover, 'I read that very same work.
Wasn't it called *From Heather and Thistle, To The Sharper Cacti Of Texas?*

'Though an excellent introduction to this mighty state, it was rather a long title.'

'Indeed, he may ramble on, but Theo has strict moral principles.
He objected to allowing that famed woodsman into our celestial domain.
You know the one, Davy Crockett, a 'hero' of the Alamo.

'He received a swift rebuff – why, the damn fellow kept a personal slave!'

Johnson interrupted, 'I love hearing you prevaricate,
your voice is like a ship's horn blaring through fog,
but my little mutt needs to find suitable cacti on which to cock its leg...'

'....You're right, I must shut my big gob, as they say in county Wicklow.
Anyway, the wind's getting stronger, and my ghostly form will dissipate,
and I've a message for you.

'Do you remember your sworn enemy, O'Toole The Terrible?'

'Indeed,' replied Johnson, 'I remember that fool Lord Hoppit-Houghton, boasting he would raise a glass when O'Toole danced the hangman's hornpipe.'

He laughed, 'Instead the pompous twit fell under his horse
at the Ballymuggin steeplechase, the silly old fool.'

'Yes well, never mind mocking our military commanders,' she smirked.
You'll be laughing at Wellington next – why the old lech made
a pass at my mother, but he wasn't her type!

'Where was I? Oh yes, O'Toole's written you a little poem.'

To The Man Who Bested Me, Ireland's Best Ever Rebel.

You were a brave fighter and a clever strategist,
whom I often wished I had on the end of my pitchfork.
But you saw the light and let peace enter your soul,
travelling across this mighty land, seeking a peaceful haven,
braving savages, pestilence and the occasional dust bowl.

So to sum up, sorry it's so short, as I am not used to this writing lark,
especially with rhyming cutlets, and I've an appointment with a glass of stout,
served by Nancy, the barmaid of The Saint And Sinner, in our little pub in Heaven.

Abandon your mission for that sod Cockslip,
whose spies were the death of me and my band,
or his machinations will see your bones rotting in the Mexican sand.

'And at the bottom of the poem he's written...'
'*Not a bad effort, though the rhymes are a bit contrived,*
but I'm too drunk to do it again.

'I'm having lessons from that chap Wordsworth, you know,
who says I could have been a writer of verse, instead of a rebel.'

After the apparition evaporated, Johnson mused. 'Was this a dream?
Fiona died in India after she married that blasted colonel,
who made my life hell, when I was a subaltern.'

The following day sheriff Pete called in Ma Murphy's Pie Pantry
and met an English chap, who got his back up with the comment,
'This sure is a one-horse town... hmm, this pie is lovely,
I was expecting it to be inedible.

'Tell me, have you seen a tall chap who arrived here in '41'.
He's a master of disguise...'

But the lawman hastily interrupted his flow,
'In that case, how would I know him?'

'Quite,' the stranger replied, 'he could say he's a Lithuanian barber
or a railwayman from Chicago, and appear perfectly credible.

'But he is also very handy with his fists, and your deputy,
who likes his whisky, remembers a well spoken chap
knocking out some fellow called Mad Mags McNoon.'

'Oh,' laughed the sheriff, 'you shouldn't listen to him,
he was probably pished.'

Making his excuses, Pete galloped away to find O'Pouncy,
convinced he'd met his friend's spymaster.

But the old shack was bare of any belongings or person.

Then a little dog appeared out of the twilight,
followed by a ragged shape wearing a broad-brimmed hat
and a ridiculously long moustache – it was Johnson,
dressed as a Mexican.

At first Pete didn't recognise him, being so artfully moustachioed.

'Old friend,' Johnson said tearfully, 'I know what you're going to say,
my old boss is here (little Cactus sniffed his scent from miles away),

and that conniving spy master has doubtless
lined up another dangerous assignment.

'Give me the location of those outlaws you came up against,
for with my secret-agent skills I can be invaluable to them.

'You mean Butch Cassidy And The Sundance Kid?

They're hiding in Cutaway Canyon.
'They owe me a favour or two, and will certainly help you vanish.'

Years later a Harvard professor, writing a book on the 'Old West',
discovered that a third 'Bandito', said to have been active in the
South American country of Bolivia, was rumoured to have operated
with the above-mentioned outlaws, who, after robbing a bank in the
city of Vallomanadid, died in an ambush.

He was said to have lived alone with a little dog,
under the name Muncy McDevitt,
and could sing and play the piano, delighting the emigrants with
his version of Stephen Foster's *Old Folks Of Home,*
but in his cups would ramble on about Lady Fulsome-Fultitude,
whom he saw in an apparition.

But all trace of him was lost in 1870,
after the visit of a Bolivian detective.

In his book, '*The British Traitor*, former Intelligence boss
Chrispin Cockslip made the outrageous claim that an English secret agent
rode with those notorious outlaws,
Butch Cassidy And The Sundance Kid.

He claimed this fellow was called Johnson O'Pouncy,
and was such a master of disguise, that even the famed detectives,
Pinkertons, don't know where he's hid.

Ah, but that's another story.

Little Lucy

Little Lucy was a hit on the South American city of
Guatemala's shanty-town cabaret,
somersaulting across the stage singing,
'I was raised in the shadow of Mount Montezuma,
and am proud to call myself by my native name,
Lucian Allamandas, the last remaining Guatemalan Apache Indian.'

'As a girl,' she declared to travelling musician Monty Bullingham,
whom she met when they shared a dense thorny bush,
hiding from baton-wielding police.

'I was known as the Singing Socialist Thief,
as I always sang *The Red Flag* – after all it is the
poor people's anthem – before visiting
the wealthy Latin Quarter and leaving with a load of swag.'

But she left her wayward ways behind, when Monty enlisted her as a roadie,
with touring band Silvery Shannon, and this naive young woman had great
fun with this interesting fellow, who'd saved her from a life of crime.

But he left her for lead singer, famed accordionist Squeezebox Sharon,
when she cashed in on the environmental wave by having a
hit with the song *Let's Protect Galway Bay,*
sung to the tune of a traditional ballad.

Lucy coped with the heartache by busking in the marketplace,
praying in the old catholic church,
playing the charango and ukulele, belting out blues classic
My Wife's Left Me In The Lurch, So Why Am I So Sad?

But using her knowledge of South America's remote mountains,
she was soon enjoying life as a mountain guide,
leading wealthy Americans into the high peaks.

One morning, gathered in the foyer of the luxurious Hilton Hotel,
she addressed such a party, 'You've engaged me to lead you into the hills,
where we'll watch soaring eagles and mountain lions,
camp by silvery streams and bathe under the mighty Wicker Waterfall.

'But if there's is any lewdness in the dark retreats
of the night – oh, I know my English poetry, I'm particularly fond of that
notorious lech Lord Byron – if I see any of that behaviour,
your lives will be forfeit,' and here she looked at the loudest of the group,
Walter Windblown-Whipflop, 'yes, I know there's no depravity to which you
imperialists wouldn't stoop.'

But high on the Falateu Plateau, Whipflop, who'd been fondling the
female bearers all through the trek, was now about to divert his attention
towards Lucy, when he was stopped by handsome New Yorker, Larry Lapitup.

Thus in one foolish night of passion she fell into his carefully-laid trap.

Alas, she soon learned that her lover was not a wealthy,
lustful American called Larry, but a cunning Cuban called Fadirous,
and headed that feared organisation, whispered among the slums of the barrios
– the Communist International, so called defenders of an oppressed people.

Trained in the art of subterfuge and sexual blackmail,
she was soon under his control, running guns to Castro on his island of Cuba,
avoiding the US Navy in the Caribbean.

Having proved her espionage qualities she was sent to Las Vegas,
as a thorn in the side of capitalism, adopting the pseudonym
of leading artist Magdalena Montague,
basking in the success of her headline-grabbing art exhibition in Paris.

There this former slum girl attracted admiring glances,
saying, 'Have a nice day' and 'Hey you're all'.

However, CIA rookie field agent Ronald Roughitup
felt there was something about her that didn't quite ring true.

Was it her exaggerated Texan drawl or playing that little guitar, the charango,
even a neat right hook that sent an over-ardent fan bottom over what's it,
or her well-thumbed copy of Karl Marx's *Das Kapital*?

Using the skills gained in the CIA methods of seduction course,
he charmed his way to her hotel bedroom,
playing the mummy's boy to the hilt,
saying he was brought up according to Biblical teaching,
and was a true innocent.

So when she invited him for a nightcap,
not only was he already dreaming of imminent copulation,
but also his subsequent rise through the agency,
as the guy who'd saved the country by his diligent intelligence work,

For he was none other than nervous Ron, a lowly field agent,
never trusted with an important mission, but always good for a laugh.

So he was deflated in more ways than one when the object of his lust
gave him a blanket and a *Bible,* and said, 'You can sleep in the bath.'

With his head on a sponge, Ron cursed as he stubbed his toe on the faucet.
However his angry heart was soon subdued by a beautiful voice
singing a mystical prayer in a strange tongue,
which he included in an in-depth report.

But when it was dismissed as 'romantic rubbish', he felt low as a skunk,
and cursed his patronising boss, the pompous Colonel Bob Bilton-Blowit.

The next day Miss Montague was approached by a young woman,
who asked her, 'Hey, can you help me with a roll of the dice,
as I'm new to this game of chance?', and she spent all day
with this new friend who called herself called Prue short
or Prudence (even though she did appear a bit manly).

That evening she and her new friend bonded, sleeping out under the stars,
and though a police patrol, alerted by Colonel Blowit to

look for a wayward secret agent, noticed Prue shaving
behind some convenient cacti, they dismissed it as,
'You get all sorts in Texas, it's this new policy of the governor's,
he's a progressive leftie'.

But, though happy away from the false, material world of Vegas,
Lucy noticed with alarm a strange attraction to this young person,
and wondered if she'd suddenly become, God forbid, a lesbian.

The next evening as she sang Bob Dylan's *I'll Keep It With Mine*,
Willie Nelson's *All The World's A Circus* and Scottish lament,
Flowers Of The Forest, Prue tipsily danced around a cactus,
slipped and was pierced on her behind.

When Lucy offered to inspect the wound, Prue declared,
'Oh, I'll have to come clean, and when I take off my wig and filled-out bra,
you'll see I'm actually a guy, and will recognise me as the chap you,
not so long ago, consigned to the bathroom,
and I know you're not who you say you are.

'But rather than being a sophisticated siren, you are Luciana Lamatandas,
the last remaining Guatemalan Apache Indian.'

When he got down on one knee, declaring, 'I'm in love with you!',
Lucy gasped, then asked, 'Is that Ron speaking, or Prue?'

A year later after a series of events too complicated for this short report,
those extremists who'd used a young woman's innocence for political gain,
along with the US militarists who'd cast her as the enemy incarnate,
heard she'd been offered a government amnesty, arranged through her lover,
an ex-government agent – in return for not spilling the beans on illegal CIA
activity.

At a press conference to publicise Ron's book,
Walking A Crooked Path – Confessions Of A Failed Spy,
everybody chuckled when Lucy described how she'd
made her husband-to-be sleep in the bath.

She then announced that, instead of remaining sworn enemies of each other,
the pair had 'buried the hatchet', so to speak (Lucy fielding an actual one,
donated by her relatives in the greater tribe Apache).

And when right-wing TV host Laurence Miles McCracken
invited Lucy on his show, The Voice Of America,
then accused her 'Of seducing a naive young American,'
everyone gasped when the man himself, Ron,
jumped onto the stage, shouting,
'I swore an allegiance to a president who
espouses an America-first policy,
but by doing so he's leaving common humanity a good second.

'So I left that life behind, when I donned a skirt and pretended to be a female,
swinging my ass around the casino, just so I could fall in love with a former
slum girl.

'So together we issue a joint snub to those militarists in Washington,
with their greed-is-best economics, including a hatred of
that cigar-smoking Fidel Castro,
and his revolutionaries with their evocation of Marx's theory of dialectics.'

Then, Lucy put her arms around him, saying,
'I'm tired of these big words, his dad wanted him to be a lawyer,
you know.

'Anyway, What Ron's trying to say is, 'Marry me,
Luciana Lamatandas, the last remaining Guatemalan Apache Indian!'

Little Susan

When Susan emerged from the womb, her tiny lips beamed a smile,
wide enough to light up the rain-soaked African plains.

Her mother knew she'd reared a mischievous child,
by the way she winked when sucking her thumb,
attracting envious glances when running through
the grass playing skip-along games.

But by morning's light she was studying her textbooks,
in the hut that served as a classroom,
where Susan's teacher, Father McAleef – told the pupils how neighbouring
South Africa's aspiring president, Dieter Vanderbroom,
had referred to their homeland as 'That hotbed of communism,
run by illiterate blacks'.

But she glowed with pride when the priest explained how their
little country had provided sanctuary to refugees escaping over those encircling
peaks – christened by early Lesothians as 'The Dragon's Teeth',
now known to mountaineers the world over as The Drakensbergs.

She'd marvelled when the elderly cleric told her enthralled class
how as a young man he'd left the Irish village of Dunmore East,
on a spiritual journey which saw him teach guerrillas in Guatemalan jungles,
war-ravaged refugees in Lebanon, and Eskimos torn from their homes by
melting icebergs.

The priest felt there was something magical about this little girl.
It wasn't just her amazing ability with mathematics – why,
look how fast she solved The McBurnick Equation.

But a sheltered life left her innocent, so it was no surprise
when she fell for political agitator Fergus Mogambon,
whom Susie discovered was handy with his fists.

But she followed him to the streets of South African city Durban,
and they were soon topping the apartheid police's top 10 subversives' list.

Alas, tragedy struck when her love was killed
by a plastic bullet, fired by the police,
who claimed they were protecting the public during a riot,
and with the net drawing closer she raced along the coast,
arriving in the semi-desert land of the Karoo.

Here, a farmer provided shelter among his ostriches
after she nursed one of them, a bird called Brave Beatrice,
– so named because, when a rustler tried to steal her,
she kicked him over a fence – using a potion gathered
from the Mallagotomo cactus.

But, betrayed by an informer, Susan escaped, clinging to Beatrice's neck.
The ostrich galloped to a subterranean stream into
which her grateful passenger dived,
following the Buffalo river to Port Elizabeth.

Here she joined a cruise ship bound for Liverpool
as a children's entertainer, Marvellous Millicent.

On arrival in England, in one of those curious twists of fate,
because Fr McAleef had said the city was synonymous with slavery,
she jogged along the Manchester Ship Canal, settling in England's rainy city.

Here she dallied with the affections of Doctor Frederick Freudmaster,
but scorned his expensive gifts, and when they went hill walking,
stayed in youth hostels instead of hotels.

However, he was successful in encouraging her to take up running,
and she joined him on group runs through the countryside
with Prestwich Park Puffers,
but she put their noses out by joining Manchester Harriers.

Due to her childhood experience of racing mountain lions,
Susan excelled at cross-country running and racing on the fells,
but was quite good on the track, setting a club record for the 1500 metres.

All the while she harboured an ambition to
appear on the big screen, nurtured when,
as a child in her village's makeshift cinema,
she'd watched US detective series *Kojak*,
laughing at those silent films of Buster Keaton,
but none was funnier than Charlie Chaplin playing a bumbling cop.

So, she flirted with roles as a supporting actress,
even playing a feminist version of Shylock in *The Merchant Of Venice*.

But Cupid's arrow struck once more when she starred in a
pop video for Scottish band The Naysayers',
playing a black skinhead singing classic hymn *Jerusalem*,
as the band sang their new single, *Reversal*,
casting a spell on manager Jim Junketman,
who took her to his mansion, Browbeaten Hall,
nestling on the shores of Loch Ness,
where his sweetheart cooked him an African version of haggis.

But her heart skipped a beat when a stranger appeared in the village,
claiming in a phoney American accent to be a descendant of Fiery Fantuck,
famed chieftain of those fearsome warriors, The McPeagles,
and saying 'I'm from a long line of Highlanders,
I even bought the kilt bearing the emblem of the clan.'

But her housekeeper pointed out, 'His skirt's tartan is that
of my ancestral tribe, The Mighty McSteagles,
and they're from a different glen.'

Intelligence sources revealed him to be Peter Van Der Billing,
a South African secret agent.

So, she left for London, disguised as Liberian nun Sister Mary Millercapelling,
falling in with a bunch of poets and playwrights,
and even had a fling with a circus master from Moscow,
but ran off after discovering he kept a knife-throwing mistress.

So, hoping to get a a walk-on role as an East End barmaid,
following the method-acting school of thought,
she visited the Cheeky chappie Cafe in Eastham,
where she met TV producer Bert Bittlemight,
poring over a script for new police series, *Bill And Ben*.

Renowned for picking unknowns, he cast her as detective Susie Shoegrass.
Her friends back home, watching British programmes on a little TV,
delighted in spotting their exiled country woman.

One day Fr McAleef laughed at a magazine feature
linking his 'Little Susan' with a former spy,
who'd admitted he was a member of the apartheid regime's security services.

The cleric laughed when this chap told a press conference,
'I became enamoured of Susan when I was ordered to Scotland,
to report on her movements after she'd fled there,
but my cover was blown by my inane attempts to portray an American.

'You see, I'd only joined my country's intelligence corp to impress my father, who'd talked about how his forebears the Boers had overcome the Zulus at Blood River.

'However, I came to a country largely untouched by the smear of prejudice. Whether it was the Rastafarians in Brixton or Liverpudlian Jamaicans in Toxteth, I realised the truth, that I wasn't really racist.

'Which was just as well, because I'd fallen for my quarry, who'd tickled my sense of humour, for she used the pseudonym, Sue Servicios...'

Then Susan interjected, 'I acquired it in Barcelona, it's Spanish for loo.'

The article finished by saying the couple were to be married.
Meanwhile, former South African president Dieter Vanderbroom
was cursing while reading the same story, in a care home on the dusty Karoo.

'Why,' he spluttered, 'I gave the groom his medal, after graduating from secret-agent college.'

A week later, a horde of school children gathered on the border between South Africa and Lesotho, to see a former pupil marry a man who'd once carried the baton of the apartheid police.

The groom laughed when reminded of this, saying, 'I couldn't catch her, she was too fast.'

Fr McAleef, now no longer sprightly and sporting a long white beard,
announced, 'Please welcome a former enemy of our homeland,
here to marry the first Lesothian TV star, ace detective Susie Shoegrass!'
Then all the children cheered.

Old runner's lament

A TV producer told me I didn't look like an athlete,
when I was cast as a competitor in the Middington-Fiddle
Village Big Mudder race, in an episode of that corny popular drama,
Country Constable, during which, you've guessed it,
a murder or two inevitably takes place.

'But I did once!' I protested, to no avail.

So my mind harked back to when I ran through mud so deep,
a tractor was used to extricate many a competitor,
when I slogged up hill and down dale,
not to mention fells a goat would struggle up, they were so steep.

Forgive my exaggeration, but I could shift when I was a lad.
I've done more reps and long runs than a Californian personal trainer,
you know the type, those who see running as a 'cool' fad.

I've made the first 100 in the National Cross Country,
when it was 'for real men', over nine miles.

I even ran for Oxford University, where I saw rugby players
doing 10-metre sprints and saying they were fit.
But now I've got such a belly I struggle to rise from my seat.

I have a personal best for 5,000 metres which is quite good, and perversely,
a better one at 1500, considering my best distance was long, and not middle.

So why wouldn't they let me be a TV star and run through the mud at
Middington-Fiddle?

I could have boasted in our village pub, The Bashful Bullock,
for though I'm a celebrity, if rather past my sell-by-date, I am awfully vain.

It was there I bumped into Musgrave McPhail, an old Irish comic,
who, due to his type of humour being out of fashion,
had accepted a role as a drunk in that very TV show I'd been rejected from.

'I'm surprised they don't have you saying begorrah!'
I cried, anxious to show how unbiased I was – after all,
Ireland gave us that famous BBC radio chap Terry Wogan!

Then to my chagrin, I woke to find my estate manager
had allowed that blasted TV show to be filmed in one of my properties!

But I got my own back by not letting them use the toilet.
Well, I thought, they can always think of their overblown fees!

Later, I laughed as I watched the actors struggle to the village convenience,
before packing my skis, to join Daphne Dovecott's chums in the Alpine town
of Sierre Zinal.

Daffers and I laughed about when we'd first met, and I told them how,
as a kid I'd hung around her private school,
Multchett Manor, Egham, when, after Tough Boy Williams
had called me a pansy for quoting Oscar Wilde,
I'd bet him I could convince a posh girl to be my pal.

Dammit, I was so good she even believed I was at Eton,
when I was actually from Slough, that very modern town.
But she soon worked me out, clever lass, and used to laugh when,
at Oxford I wore a hat and gown – stolen of course.

The hotel was abuzz with the fact that a movie director
was staying there, Milo Mills-Milde, responsible for such classics
as *Incident At Whitehall* – 'An assassin stalks Downing Street',
and that 'Thrilling survival epic' – *A long Way To Fall.*

It was the sequel to the latter which had brought him to our mountain retreat,
where that evening, full of brandy, Daffers was boasting about her son,
'Ever Ready Everard', who'd earned rave reviews for his one-man show,
playing a camp Shakespeare – Ballads Of The Bard,
while in the background Milo was working hard on a script.

I thought I'd puncture her pomposity, so asked,
'What did that military husband of yours think about that?
What was he called – Bunty Buffers-Buntington?
He hated anything outrageously unmasculine.'

'I know,' she laughed, 'and even though you couldn't half run,
you were rubbish at rugby or football, and, what's more,
and I quote, 'a right ponce' with that speech impediment.

'I didn't agree, of course, hence his jealousy of you.

'Don't worry, he's far away, ex-colonel Bunty's a mercenary in South Africa,
fighting the mighty Matabele.

'Or do I mean the Zulu?'

'You are joking!' I exclaimed.

'Last I heard he was running one of those adventure camps in Surrey,
£500 a day and bring your own tent.'

'Really?

'Well he always said you were a fool.

'By the way, he found the poem you wrote about me.'

'What did he think of it?'

'All he could say was, you don't know where to put the apostrophe.'

'Yes well,' I interjected, 'Slough comprehensive wasn't the best school.'

Then I felt it was time for my party piece, so I got up and quoted,
'I've come to apologise... not to you (pause) to Charles.
I've been perfectly bloody (pause) and I've come to apologise.'

Daffers laughed, saying, '*Brideshead Revisited*!

'I always loved your Sebastian.'

But later that night I cried for my lost youth,
when to escape reality I would read boys own stories,
becoming ace First World War pilot Biggles,
downing the Hun in a rickety biplane, the Sopwith Camel,
or Sir Percy Blakeney, the Scarlet Pimpernel.

This escape into another world had helped me climb, despite my stammer, into the exalted ranks of those fast-talking twits who dominate the TV panel-show circuit.

For my vivid imagination helped me quell a terrible inner fear.
But that night, as I watched my friends drink themselves to oblivion,
I realised I'd become a pastiche of myself.

But, like the characters created in *Brideshead* by Evelyn Waugh,
that posh literary soldier who encapsulated the divide in Britain,
during those years before the war, I'd refused to accept it.

So being rejected from that TV series because I didn't look like a runner was poetic justice.

Why, being an athlete was the only thing I'd found hard.
All those tough track sessions I missed through depression,
being too embarrassed to admit it, not even to an NHS therapist,
but in the theatrical world it's quite accepted, a hazard of the profession.

The next day I was approached by that movie chap, Milo,
who said, 'Didn't we run together at Oxford?'

Then I suddenly recognised him, 'Oh yes,
I remember you – Milo with the Biro,
you were always writing ideas for a film.'

‘Indeed, and I made quite a bit of money from ’em.

‘Anyway, last night I thought I knew you.
Then it hit me – you used to do that *Brideshead* quote a lot.

‘Quite amusing, but not after the 20th time.
Anyway, do you fancy a part in my movie?

‘I’m just finishing off the plot, it’s about an old runner’s reunion.

‘You’d play an old bore, suit you down to the ground,’ he said,
without even the hint of a smile.

Intrigued, I asked, ‘And what happens to this chap?’

‘He’s murdered, and this will amuse you, the chief suspect
is played by Bunty Buffers-Buntington.

‘Now, isn’t that a coincidence?

‘Did you know he’s an actor and producer on that TV detective show, *Country Constable*?’

I was astounded. ‘You mean the one where,
instead of chasing poachers and dishing out fines,
the local cop’s investigating murders?’

‘That’s right, apparently it’s based near the place we’re filming.

‘I think it’s called Middington-Muddle.

‘Sure you don’t mean Middington-Fiddle?’

‘Oh! Anyway, you’re found dead, with a copy of
Brideshead Revisited strapped to your middle.’

Little Sue and the giants

Those English mountains, Glaramara and Scafell,
which stand like mighty sentinels guarding the approaches to Cumbria's coast,
once echoed to the sound of the hairy hipnochroids, those huge horny cattle,
who with their huge teeth, made a mighty 'chomp, chomp!' noise,
chewing tough heather and thistle, then roaring 'Mac Mullett Moose Maa!',
meaning 'Our neighbours prefer us up here, as we've got bad breath'.

While below the Woolly Wignot sheep growl
'Brue Ma Muggle Miggle Ma TacGagle',
meaning 'The food's better down here, and we can see ever so far.'

Watching over these mighty beasts are a band of little girls,
who by ancient decree were appointed The Sheep And Cattle Guardians,
and, due to their amazing agility in leaping over rock and fell,
became known as the Sure-footed Susans.

Though small in stature, they easily fight off wolves and mountain tigers,
who at first think they have an easy prey, but once the chief guardian
shouts 'Magmu guddle gadabout biggle,'
they run away from this little, but tough gal.

But where there are little folk, there may also be found massive people.
One such was 'Big Lad', affectionately known thus because he was a giant,
and besides his real name was a mouthful – Ladderwackermackdidle.

One day the little Susies, seeking shelter, discovered this chap in a cave,
and, crying out in wonder, woke him from his sleep.

Though when facing ordinary mortals, they were extremely brave,

these feisty females nevertheless gave a little squeak, and one,
losing her footing, nearly fell, but a huge hairy hand
reached out and grabbed her,
and they were all soon enjoying a cup of tea.

They invited him to their hillside village of Lithermagillium,
where he soon overcame his shyness,
becoming a regular visitor to their beautiful valley.

Though at first afraid when they heard the 'Thud! Thud!' of his footsteps,
the villagers welcomed him with open arms,
and he became a common sight with his bulging biceps,
giving piggybacks to children, who sang 'Big Lad we love you'.

This became such a regularity that children had to form a disorderly queue.

However, though acquiring lots of new friends,
the giant missed out on love due to being so big,
and the fact that in times of heavy rainfall he caused
great floods when needing to 'piddle'.

So he doused his sorrows with beer, said to be legendary
warrior Mighty McMontrose's favourite tipple.

However, cruel tongues, forgetting what life was like before his arrival,
whispered about the man above, 'He's big but he's sad.'

But that all changed when he limped into the village,
battered yet triumphant, though minus a boot,
describing how he'd scared off warlike invaders.

After that the gossips wouldn't dare engage in tittle tattle,
as they heard him describe how,
hearing about an incursion into his mountain domain,
he had come upon an advance party of Roman soldiers,
whose job it was to build a fort from the oaks of Hardknott Forest,
and from there march out to slaughter and pillage.

Thus enraged, Big Lad ran amok among them,
and, after their spears failed to penetrate his tough skin,

the soldiers hurled axes, one hitting his right heel,
propelling him into a stinking bog,
causing such a splash his pursuers couldn't see through the watery mist.

But after the wind blew away this temporary veil, he was nowhere to be seen.

For unknown to his pursuers he'd lain submerged,
breathing through a hollow log, blending with the watery terrain,
a trick he'd used as a boy when hiding from flying fillinousarusses,
those huge flying reptiles that had bedevilled the area,
swooping down on goats and sheep, eventually settling on a remote island,
established as a protectorate for endangered species.

At nightfall he rose and climbed mighty peak Helvellyn,
following the drovers' path over Striding Edge,
and after a welcome sup of goat's milk from a tiny hovel,
arrived in Lithermagillium.

But, distressed to see their hero with a bare foot,
after losing his boot to a Roman axe,
the Susies found him a servant, called Tim,
who asked a leather wrangler to fashion his master some sturdy footwear.

When asked how much he wanted for this, the kind chap answered 'Nowt'.

At first the servant puzzled to understand him,
but was informed that the cobbler was from a village called Oswaldtwistlemax,
in that hilly county Lancashire, which espouses a particular dialect,
rather similar to that of Yorkshire, if you know it.

'Just mention me when your boss wears the product of
my endeavours on his huge feet,' he added.

Many years passed and the Romans left with their tails between weather beaten legs.

Then one night a wee girl called Feisty Felicity McThistle,
hearing tales of this mighty giant, followed him from a tavern,
when he suddenly sat down and fell asleep.

Then a mighty storm broke and he was washed away into the ocean,
but guided by Doris, a dolphin tasked by the Marine Master
of the Atlantic Approaches to watch out for wayward boats,
reached the safety of the Irish fishing port of Killybegs.

The wet and cold big fellow thought he was dreaming,
when Felicity appeared from his coat pocket,
which she'd leaped into, to escape the rising water.

After he'd dozed off again, she appeared with a tray of warm-buttered farls,
which is Irish bread, and of course,
being in Ireland, the obligatory pot of tay.

He thought she must be a magician, but the little lady
explained that she'd gone to a bar called the Inn Plaice,
full of fishermen, who, listening in awe to her story
– about her huge pal being a relative of an Ulster giant –
believed she must be some kind of fairy,
so quickly acquiesced to her request for tea and toast.

'This is lovely bread, and I want the recipe,' she said,
'we must contact your cousin, you know,
the one who didn't finish The Giant's Causeway
off the Coast of Antrim?'

'Oh yes!' he answered, 'He's one of my Irish relatives, Brian Borou;
wait a minute, my nursery teacher told me he was Finn McCool.

'Oh, you're right, I am a big fool.
Apparently, he was ever such a lazy chap.'

'Really?' laughed Felicity, 'Anyway, I shall call
Doris and get to her to push me with her snout,
all the way around the coast, past Rathlin Island,
with its hermitage devoted to the preservation of Gaelic tradition.

'There I shall pick up tatty pies for my lunch,
and for Doris salted herring, then complete the journey in your boot.'

Felicity was soon sailing under a cliff,
where she could hear gigantic snoring.

Fearing it was a sea monster taking a nap,
she crawled in under cover of seaweed,
and sighed with relief after seeing it was he whom she sought.

'Don't worry about your stranded Big Lad,' the curious giant said,
'I shall have him brought here by a specially-constructed coracle,
built for big fellows like him and me.'

Then, sensing he could talk to this little creature,
he unburdened himself, admitting to be very lonely.

'Though I get the occasional wave from a passing mermaid,
when I invite her on shore she's left stranded on slippery
rock and falls into the briny.

'So, I prefer to stay at home and read parchments written by hermits,'
he sobbed, 'who are very clever, but, being shy,
are much misunderstood by their fellow man, and woman.

'Actually, they're just like me.

'Anyway, would you like to meet Saint Patrick, little Felicity?

'He dishes out holy blessings for people who show kindness,
just like you have, by listening to my tales of being rejected.'

She did as asked, and that revered cleric, who rid Ireland of snakes
but later came to regret it, saying in his memoirs it
was one of his biggest mistakes,
was most impressed by this little girl,
and hearing she came from a land of bizarre beasts,
insisted they be protected.

So he dispatched Big Lad and his cousin to Cumbria,
with the words, 'Brian, say hello to Felicity's mum,
and while there help the Little Susans safeguard
these amazing animals I hear tell of.

'For I hear it was decreed by that famed holy man,
Arthur Of The Square Table, that 'As long as these mighty creatures live,
England shall remain free'.'

Brian, like his cousin Big Lad, became useful around the village,
and soon twinned the place with his birthplace of MackerMcMable,
over in Ulster.

Drawing up a plan of preservation, the little gals, helped by the giants,
herded the woolly wignots and hairy hipnochroids to a hidden vale,
where they grazed contentedly.

But when news of their hideaway became known,
the roads were soon filled by carts, full of tourists,
who, although the village animal doctor had prescribed a strict diet,
fed them the wrong food, and were distressed
when a young cow nearly swallowed a carrot.

So the Susies guided their charges by a secret passageway
to a huge underground limestone cavern known as Gaping Gill.

There the Wignots feasted on a plentiful supply of grass,
muttering, 'Bag boog justin saddington happernot twiddle loffalot fagoid,'
meaning 'It's nice here, and the cows are eating healthier undergrowth,
resulting in much nicer breath.'

'Thanks, we heartily agree,' said the chief hipnochroid.

So Felicity, the little girls and their giant pals retired
in the knowledge that these bizarre beasts would be safe,
and indeed, they are there still.

Little Stan The Referee

My grandad started watching rugby league
after returning to St Helens from war-torn France,
and was heard to remark, 'They breed 'em tough in Lancashire.'

He'd watched in awe as Albert Briggins,
a towering prop forward, cowered before little referee,
Stanley Smiggins who, as a spy in the Great War,
had led the Hun on a merry dance,
and was now calmly reprimanding the huge Wigan player.

Stan's mates – who'd known him since school,
and had often ribbed the little chap about his ambition to play rugby,
saying, 'Tha's too small, you little wimp, go down the mines
like us and dig coal!' – now marvelled at his nerve.
After all, he was only a little lad.

So when trouble brewed during that game,
the little ref calmly wagged his finger at Albert,
even though he could easily have shut him up.
For, like all secret agents, Stan was a karate expert.

Then, after they'd all trooped off, Mrs Lovebody, a staunch Wigan supporter,
incensed that Stan had sent Bert into the sheds for an early bath,
hit him on the bonce with her umbrella.

My granddad, Joe was there that day with his sons, John, Bill and Gerry,
and told the tale over a pint at the Smiggins Arms,
named in honour of Stan, the ex-secret agent and rugby league referee.

Due to the exigency of the Official Secrets Act,
our heroic ref never talked about his espionage
activities in that terrible conflict.

Though in the corridors of power he was known as the greatest of spies,
he would escape to the loo when asked what he'd done in the war.
For unlike some so-called tough guys,
he was possessed of considerable tact,
but rather lamented he'd never represented his
home town in the greatest game of all.

But his bravery shone through as the little chap
who kept order with just his whistle,
among the big men who kick and pass the oval ball.

Beach boy

People scoff when I dig out my old reviews to boost a fading ego,
but I boast to my contemporaries that's there was no one like me,
that old star of stage and screen, who almost became the 'fifth' Beatle.
Ah, but that's another story.

As an actor, it hurt that some regarded me as a one-trick pony.
For, being a handsome devil, I was often cast
as the romantic lead in our drama school plays.

I was admired by that new generation of performers, the 'theatrical gays',
and even dabbled with that scene; but they soon recognised me as a phoney.

My care home is full of annoying people, like 'Major' Montague,
always talking of some bloody battle, and former pop star Gladys Goodworthy,
trying to remember her hit single.

But I've lately teamed up with a former film critic and fellow resident,
'Dashing' Dave Dovecot, notorious in Fleet Street as an old soak.

I've forgiven him for his critical reviews of my cinematic roles,
as he lets me join him behind the care home bike shed,
where we smoke weed, and when I'm 'high',
I imagine being welcomed under God's Pearly Gate for doing what for me,
was a rare act of kindness.

This occurred on a beach where the British Army would
have faced the Nazi hordes, in those dark days of 1940.
It was there that I found a shivering boy, who resembled me in his
precociousness.

Dave and I took him for a barge trip on the Norfolk Broads,
and one day I asked, 'How did you end up on that beach in Kent,
little black man?' after we'd listened to him read poems and soliloquies to rival
any young thespian.

'Oh, I landed on a leaky boat,' he nervously admitted,
'but that won't stop me becoming a great actor, will it?

'I mean, not actually being who I say I am?'

At this plea I laughed fit to burst.
'Oh, don't worry about that, nobody's a bigger fake than me,
and I'm your biggest fan, in fact, I predict you'll be a star.'

'In that case I'll be able to afford to bring my parents here.

'They could do with a break from the horror of civil war,
and can I play footie with that former football great, Gary Linebreaking?

'We used to watch him score goals for fun,
on telly in my poverty-stricken township, playing for Man United,
or am I thinking of that fellow Beckendatin?

'Gary's no fool when it comes to speaking his mind,
and standing up for those who flee a war-torn land.'

Impressed by this response, I could only add,
'Indeed, young man, in fact I think I met the fellow,
on a BBC promo I did for £50, cash in hand.

'He didn't mind at all when I admitted to not liking football,
and laughed at my story of how I almost became the fifth Beatle.

'Why, he even called me a funny old fart, thinking that was a theatrical term of
endearment.'

‘Oh, do tell me that Beatle story,’ my youthful new pal asked, ‘I want to absorb British culture.’

‘I wouldn’t bother, dear boy, the world I knew has gone to hell in a hand cart, but I’m glad to say a young chap like you has given me fresh hope.

‘You’re like a newly discovered star in the heavenly firmament.’

I’ve heard that the beach boy is now lighting up Hollywood, though the US Border Force have found evidence he’s not who he says he is.

His response was, ‘Didn’t the people who discovered America arrive on a leaky boat?’

www.ingramcontent.com/pod-product-compliance
Lightning Source LLC
LaVergne TN
LVHW041030150826
845672LV00001B/249

* 9 7 8 8 1 1 9 6 5 4 9 6 3 *